John Bunyan's

The Pilgrim's Progress Companion

Includes Study Guide, Historical Context, Biography, and Character Index

BookCaps™ Study Guides

www.bookcaps.com

Cover Image © Tyler Olson - Fotolia.com

© 2013. All Rights Reserved.

Table of Contents

HISTORICAL CONTEXT 4

PLOT SUMMARY 8

KEY CONCEPTS 13

    THE ILLUSION OF THIS WORLD AND THE GLORY OF THE WORLD TO COME 13
    THE IMPORTANCE OF DIVINE GRACE (THE WICKET GATE) ... 14
    THE BURDEN OF SIN AND THE EFFICACY OF THE CROSS 15
    THE POWER AND IMPORTANCE OF FAITH 16
    THE GUIDANCE, PROTECTION, AND CARE OF THE LORD OF THE WAY 17
    STAYING ON THE PATH AND THE VALUE OF A GUIDE 18
    THE MISSION OF THE STRONG TO HELP THE WEAK 19
    THE MISSION TO DESTROY EVIL 20
    GIVING INCREASES, WHILE WITHHOLDING DIMINISHES 21
    THE HUMBLE SHALL BE EXALTED, AND THE PROUD SHALL BE BROUGHT LOW 22

KEY PEOPLE 23

    CHRISTIAN 23
    FAITHFUL 24
    HOPEFUL 24
    GOODWILL, THE KEEPER OF THE WICKET GATE 25
    THE INTERPRETER 25
    CHRISTIANA, MERCY, AND CHRISTIANA'S FOUR BOYS 26
    GREAT-HEART 26
    HONEST, VALIANT-FOR-TRUTH, AND STANDFAST 27
    FEARING, FEEBLE-MIND, AND READY-TO-HALT 28
    GIANT DESPAIR 28
    THE SHEPHERDS AND THE SHINING ONES 29
    THE LORD OF THE WAY, THE HILL, AND THE CELESTIAL CITY 29

BOOK SUMMARY 31

OPENING APOLOGY	32
PART I	36
PART II: INTRODUCTION	112
PART II	**117**
ABOUT BOOKCAPS	**195**

Historical Context

Birth and childhood—John Bunyan (1628-1688) was born in Elstow, England, a village near Bedford. Though his father was a tinker (someone who fixed metal utensils), and despite Bunyan's own assessment that they were terribly poor, his family appears to have been relatively well-off for that profession, judging from the fact that they lived in their own home rather than traveling, like most tinkers. Largely self-taught, Bunyan learned the basics of reading and writing in school. One aspect of his early life that is repeatedly mentioned as significant are his dreams of fiends and devils, though he had an otherwise happy childhood.

Major events of the period—The time period in which Bunyan lived was a difficult one. Aside from Civil War, there was also widespread religious intolerance and persecution and an unstable government that eventually reinstated the monarchy in 1660, after a period under the Cromwell Protectorate. That brought with it a return to severe religious intolerance as the Church of England attempted once again to dominate the religious landscape. In 1664, London experienced a two-year outbreak of the plague, to be immediately followed by the Great Fire in 1666.

Dramatic life changes—The Civil War period proved to be a personally dramatic, tragic, and destabilizing one for Bunyan despite the fact that, although he was drafted, he may never have been involved in the fighting. Aside from the deaths of his mother and sister, there was also his father's remarriage, not to mention a host of new and sometimes strange and tempting ideas to which the young man found himself exposed. When the war ended, Bunyan settled back in Elstow, where he took up his father's profession and two years later married the woman (name unknown) who eventually bore him four children. Her sole dowry consisted of two religious books, of which one, *The Plain Man's Pathway to Heaven,* was one of the precursors in style to *The Pilgrim's Progress.*

Spiritual influences—The spiritual change of heart apparently precipitated by the congenital blindness of Bunyan's first child, Mary, in 1650, ultimately led to his role as deacon of St. John's, the Baptist Church in Bedford. The nonconformist minister of that church, John Gifford, played a deciding role in Bunyan's life, in part because of his own conversion from extreme sinner to reformed preacher, something with which Bunyan could identify, since he considered himself the worst of all sinners. Gifford was the inspiration for the character of the Evangelist in *The Pilgrim's Progress.* Bunyan was also deeply affected by Martin Luther's *Commentary on the Epistle to the Galatians,* which deals with the issue of the law versus Divine Grace.

Preaching and initial writings—Shortly after becoming deacon in 1655, Bunyan began to extend his preaching activities outside the church and to add the written word to his means of communication. His first written work in 1656, a treatise against the Quakers called *Some Gospel Truths Opened,* was followed by a defense of the same work a year later, after protests from the Quakers, whose beliefs in an inner light and the inherent good in all mankind did not sit well with Bunyan. The character Ignorance in the first part of *The Pilgrim's Progress* is thought to be based on Bunyan's concept of Quaker beliefs.

Imprisonment for nonconformist religious activities—Bunyan remarried following the death of his first wife in 1658. When the monarchy was reinstated in 1660, he was jailed for organizing meetings and preaching along nonconformist lines, against the teachings of the dominant Church of England. His new wife, Elizabeth, tried unsuccessfully to have him released from a jail sentence that had begun as a three-month stint but then grew into a twelve-year incarceration. While in jail, he wrote prolifically and made bootlaces as a means of earning his family's keep. It was during this period that Bunyan wrote *The Pilgrim's Progress.*

Release from prison and success as a preacher and author—In 1672, twelve years after his initial imprisonment, Bunyan was made pastor of St. John's upon the death of the previous pastor, John Whiteman (Gifford had died much earlier, in 1655). Six years later, *The Pilgrim's Progress* was published to considerable acclaim and ongoing success. By this time, Bunyan was a widely known and respected pastor with a steady literary output. This was also the era of Milton's *Paradise Lost,* published roughly ten years earlier in 1667, and to which *The Pilgrim's Progress* has been compared in some ways, being described as a poor man's version. In 1685, Bunyan bequeathed all his goods to his family for fear of ongoing religious persecution. Three years later, he caught pneumonia and died after riding horseback in the rain to help resolve another family's dispute. Shortly after his death, William of Orange invaded England, resulting in the flight of James II and the subsequent coronation of William and Mary. This apparently opened the way to the publication of Bunyan's remaining works.

Plot Summary

An allegory of an allegory—It is clear from the beginning that John Bunyan's work *The Pilgrim's Progress* is an allegory. The characters, landscapes, and buildings, as wells as other stops along the Way, all signify mental and spiritual ideas that ultimately, either positively or negatively, point toward the final goal of redemption and awakening to an eternal, glorified existence, the pilgrims' true home and state of being. Similarly, the characters' actions and reactions illustrate the progress of those who choose to embark on this journey—the trials, pitfalls, missteps, victories, guidance, and concrete help they experience. What is perhaps not so obvious is that the story can be viewed as an allegory of an allegory, that the dream is a reference to the illusory condition that most of us believe to be the real world, the material existence that surrounds us and takes up most of our time and thoughts. Bunyan partly illustrates this through the narration of the story from a dream state and partly from the story itself, which repeatedly leads away from the empty distractions of this world to the perfect, joyful reality of the "world to come."

The two books—The plot is divided into two basic sections: Christian's awakening to his need for redemption and his subsequent pilgrimage to the Celestial City; and following that, his wife Christiana and their children's pilgrimage, together with their companion Mercy. The specific characters they meet, and the incidents that befall them are too numerous to fully outline here, and though their journeys bear some similarities, there are also striking differences.

The overall outline as it applies to both journeys involves:

- an awakening to the horrible burden of sin and the recognition of the need for redemption beyond their own efforts
- the determination to make the pilgrimage from the City of Destruction to the Celestial City
- the Slough of Despond
- the Wicket Gate, the only legitimate starting point onto the true Way, and the meeting with the Keeper of the Gate
- Beelzebub's castle
- the Interpreter's House, the first stopping place for rest and guidance along the Way
- the Cross and the Sepulchre, where Christian finally lost his burden of sin and where all true pilgrims experience a sense of profound recognition and gratitude
- Simple, Sloth, and Presumption, the three sleeping men, later the three hanged men

- the Hill Difficulty, including the two false paths at its base (though they were fenced off by the time of Christiana's arrival), the Lord's Arbor, the lions, and the House Beautiful
- the Valley of Humiliation
- the Valley of the Shadow of Death
- the giants by the cave
- the town of Vanity and Vanity Fair
- the Plain Ease with the Hill Lucre and its Silver Mine
- the Pillar of Salt
- the River of the Water of Life
- By-Path Meadow, with the style leading to Doubting Castle, home of the Giant Despair and his wife Diffidence
- the Delectable Mountains, with a clear view of the Celestial Gate
- the By-way to Hell
- the Enchanted Ground
- the land Beulah, a perfect land of perpetual light, with orchards and vineyards, and because it bordered the Celestial Country, with frequent visits from the Shining Ones
- the River with no bridge
- the hill leading to the Celestial Gate
- the Celestial Gate and the Celestial City

The main differences between the two journeys are as follows:

- Christian was either alone or with only one other person, whereas Christiana's group consisted of at least six people.
- Christiana's group had a guide for much of the journey, while Christian had only intermittent guidance.
- Christian traveled in the dark in places where the second group had light (except later, in the Enchanted Ground area, where the reverse was true).
- Christian's way was beset by difficulties that were spared Christiana's group, in part because they were women and children but also because they followed their guide closely and avoided some of the mistakes Christian had made; because Christian's earlier pilgrimage paved the way for their own, and because Great-heart, the guide for Christiana's group, either vanquished or frightened off the different evil beings along the route.
- Christiana's group had more resting places (inns and homes) than Christian and his companions.
- Christiana's journey apparently took much longer, largely because they stayed in certain places for long periods of time.
- Although both groups met many of the same characters, there were differences. The principle here seems to be that because the Way is a type of training and purification in preparation for entrance into the Celestial City, some of its specifics are tailored to individual or individuals, both in terms of past deeds and current ability.

In both cases, there were requirements for authentication, such as certificates and letters, which were received either through special messengers or at key places along the Way. The presence of the Lord of the Way all along the route is also evident in the special lodgings and arbors that he builds for his pilgrims as well as through different characters, many of whom seem to represent Christ in some form.

Key Concepts

The illusion of this world and the glory of the world to come

Bunyan's *The Pilgrim's Progress* is an allegory about spiritual pilgrimage through the difficulties and temptations of this world toward the attainment of a higher state—the eternal, true, and glorious state of being commonly called "heaven." The things of this world are considered illusive and tending only toward destruction, unable to bring true happiness, peace, or fulfillment. By contrast, the things of the "world to come" are characterized by light, perfection, and joy, and their pursuit through careful, guided pilgrimage—no matter how dark and dangerous the way—leads to increased health, happiness, and peace. The narrative is told from a dream state, further underscoring the illusive nature of this world.

The importance of Divine Grace (the Wicket Gate)

The importance of entering the Way through the Wicket Gate is illustrated by 1) the need for a Certificate of authenticity to enter the Celestial City and 2) the fruitlessness of the efforts of those who enter the Way from various side paths. In Bunyan's depiction, such pilgrims are always instantly transported to hell on reaching the Celestial Gate, as are those without a Certificate or Letter verifying their genuineness. The insistence that all pilgrims must enter through the Gate to gain access to the Way points to such Christly sayings as: "I am the way, the truth, and the life: no man cometh unto the Father, but by me" (John 14:6) and "Enter ye in at the strait gate: for wide *is* the gate, and broad *is* the way, that leadeth to destruction, and many there be which go in thereat" (Matthew 7:13).

The burden of sin and the efficacy of the Cross

As a child, Bunyan was haunted by dreams of demons and, as a young man, by his own sinfulness. Though he went through a period where he made significant changes to his outward lifestyle, he still did not feel that he could shed the heavy burden of guilt and sin. From the start, Christian is portrayed as carrying a burden on his back, making his pilgrimage wearisome until he finally encounters the Cross, when his burden falls off his back and into the nearby sepulchre. This is a statement about the innate sinfulness of man and his inability to shed his burden through his own efforts. For this, he needs the gift of Divine Grace, the redemption of his own nature through Christ's sacrifice on the Cross.

The power and importance of Faith

Closely allied to the notion of redemption through Christ's sacrifice is the importance of Faith, especially as opposed to the idea that man can redeem himself through his own inner light or works. Bunyan, however, did not share the antinomian point of view that justification by faith implied a person's license to do whatever he or she pleased. Quite the contrary, it assumed a higher level of virtue that went beyond mere outward expressions of goodness and morality to include the whole person, inside and out. Faith was also an important element for the journey itself, as demonstrated by the difference between Christian's and Hopeful's experiences of the River with no bridge, where Hopeful, because of his faith, found immediate solid footing, while Christian struggled to avoid drowning.

The guidance, protection, and care of the Lord of the Way

All along the Way are resting places built by the Lord of the Way for the refreshment and instruction of pilgrims. They are mostly in the form of houses and arbors but also include meadows, orchards, and vineyards so that the weary may nourish and heal themselves. Guidance and protection also comes in the form of human guides outside of the houses and other specified areas—guides such as Evangelist and Great-heart, who steer the pilgrims in the right direction. Those within the houses and areas such as the Delectable Mountains have the function of preparing the pilgrims through instruction and supplying them with provisions for the next leg of their journey. The Lord of the Way has also been known to adjust the circumstances of the path to the abilities of the different pilgrims, in addition to supplying a lack or desire seemingly out of the blue.

Staying on the path and the value of a guide

One of the essential elements of a successful pilgrimage is the need to adhere closely to the true path. Deviating in any way inevitably leads to more trouble than it is worth. The difficulty is that the alternate path often looks easier or more attractive at first, but it always leads to treacherous or fatal territory. Staying on the original path does not guarantee an easy or pleasant time, but in the long run, it is the safest and surest of all choices. The main purpose of the Lord's Way is to purify and prepare the pilgrim for entry into the Celestial City.

The mission of the strong to help the weak

Christianity is not a religion of the survival of the fittest. The poor, the infirm, the weak, the old, and the young are by no means left behind. In fact, weakness, if approached correctly, can become a strength if it forces the person to rely on the power of God rather than his or her own strength. However, understanding the weaknesses and fears of human nature, the Lord of the Way also commissions those who are humanly strong to guide and protect their weaker brothers and sisters. And at different places along the path, Christ himself appears to perform exactly that function, as in the instance of the Good Shepherd who tends the lambs and cares for the small children.

The mission to destroy evil

In *The Pilgrim's Progress,* there are three categories of evil: 1) the sinfulness that the pilgrim finds within himself, often most painfully at the beginning of his journey; 2) the waywardness of the false or misguided pilgrim; and 3) the evil resident along the Way, which has the specific purpose of preventing pilgrims from reaching the Celestial City, often totally destroying them. The first is destroyed through the workings of Divine Grace and the pilgrim's faithful adherence to the Way and its teachings. The second is self-destroyed through its own waywardness, either by taking a fatal detour or being rejected at the Celestial Gate and sent to Hell. The third, however, as in the destruction of Doubting Castle and the Giant Despair, requires a special effort on the part of a strong and wise human being, such as Great-heart, who is especially commissioned for that purpose.

Giving increases, while withholding diminishes

The concept that giving increases and withholding diminishes is best expressed through the characters of Gaius and Mercy. Gaius, the innkeeper, does not charge pilgrims for their room and board at his inn. Instead, he waits for his payment from the Good Samaritan—in this case, an apparent reference to Christ—who will reimburse him on his return. Being an innkeeper and thus exposed to many different people, Gaius has had ample opportunity to observe this principle in action and has noticed that giving indeed tends toward increase, while a comparable self-interest diminishes, ultimately making the person poor. Like Gaius, Mercy is constantly extending herself to others, especially the poor, for whom she endlessly spends her time sewing clothing.

The humble shall be exalted, and the proud shall be brought low

This is another example of how the laws of heaven are the reverse of the laws of this world. In *The Pilgrim's Progress,* it is most vividly illustrated by the pilgrim's varying experiences in the Valley of Humiliation, where Christian struggled in violent battle with Apollyon, the dragonlike fiend of destruction, while Mercy and Mr. Fearing, who always put others first, felt comfortable—in Fearing's case, even happy—and at home. Fearing, also, who saw himself as unworthy of entering through the Wicket Gate and preferred to let others in first, was finally lifted up by the Gatekeeper himself, who invited him to enter.

Key People

Christian

The main character of the first part, Christian represents what Bunyan held to be a true Christian, one who understands the workings of Divine Grace and practices Christian virtues and a Christlike life from the inside out through the power of God. He constantly resists the temptations and illusions of this world and strives to adhere to the true Way that leads to the Celestial Gate, though, at times, he slips and runs into trouble.

Faithful

Christian's companion for most of the first section of his journey, Faithful ends up dying a horrible death at Vanity Fair, the archetypal representation of human vanity and depravity. Faithful's valiant martyrdom, however, serves to convert some of the town's inhabitants and to moderate the actions and attitudes of many others so that by the time Christiana and her group arrive, the environment is much more hospitable to pilgrims.

Hopeful

Christian's companion for the second part of his journey, Hopeful was one of the inhabitants of the town of Vanity who was deeply affected and converted by Faithful's martyrdom. He stays with Christian to the very end, and their mutual support along the Way is a key to their success.

Goodwill, the Keeper of the Wicket Gate

The Keeper of the Wicket Gate appears to represent Christ, though Bunyan never actually says so. He is the person who answers those who knock at the Gate, asking them about their origins and intentions. He is especially kind and gentle toward the fearful and the weak, and without his Certificate, no one can enter through the Celestial Gate.

The Interpreter

The Interpreter's House is one of the early stopping places along the Way. It is also a place of instruction, where pilgrims are shown different scenes, most of which serve as warnings against pitfalls. Like the Gatekeeper, the Interpreter is sensitive to the needs of weaker pilgrims, such as extra guidance and protection or special care and provisions.

Christiana, Mercy, and Christiana's four boys

Christiana is Christian's wife and one of the main characters of the second part of *The Pilgrim's Progress*. After opposing his pilgrimage and resisting his attempts to convert her, she undergoes the same conversion by Divine Grace that Christian experienced, which leads her to follow in his footsteps. She is accompanied from the beginning by her four sons, Matthew, Samuel, Joseph, and James, and by a young woman named Mercy, who is moved to go with her.

Great-heart

Great-heart is the appointed guide who accompanies Christiana's party from the Interpreter's house all the way to the River before the hill leading to the Celestial City. He is an experienced guide who has led many pilgrims, instructing them and keeping them safe from harm. He has a mission to destroy evil and protect and help the weak, and his prowess with the sword ensures the safety of those he leads. As an allegorical figure, Great-heart represents the minister who guides his flock.

Honest, Valiant-for-Truth, and Standfast

Honest, a staunch elderly pilgrim who had been on the path for some time, was found sleeping by the wayside by Great-heart and joined the party from that point on. Valiant-for-truth, who had been assaulted by three men and was in a severely bloodied condition, was also met with along the way by Christiana's party toward the end of the journey. He helped Great-heart escort the party safely to the land of Beulah, just before the River and the hill leading to the Celestial Gate. Even farther along, at the end of the Enchanted Ground, the party met Standfast as he was praying for deliverance from Madam Bubble, the sorceress to tried to distract pilgrims with the things of this world. All three pilgrims made it to the Celestial City.

Fearing, Feeble-mind, and Ready-to-halt

Fearing, Feeble-mind, and Ready-to-halt are three examples of weaker pilgrims who nevertheless made it all the way to the Celestial City, with the help and protection of Great-heart. Fearing made the pilgrimage earlier, as we learn from Great-heart's recounting of their journey together. Feeble-mind was rescued by Great-heart from the clutches of the Giant Slay-good, and just as he was wishing for appropriate company for what he feared was too slow a pace, along came Ready-to-halt on his crutches. Again, all three, with the help of Great-heart and the others, made it all the way to the Celestial City.

Giant Despair

Although there are many evil and wayward characters in both parts of *The Pilgrim's Progress,* the Giant Despair is one of the more prominent ones. He and his wife Diffidence inhabit Doubting Castle, where they imprison pilgrims who have strayed into their territory, torturing them and starving them to death. Both the giant and his wife, along with their castle, are finally destroyed by Great-heart with the help of Honest and Christiana's four grown sons.

The Shepherds and the Shining Ones

The Shepherds are the last of the stationary guides. They reside in the Delectable Mountains, which have a view of the Celestial City, and they instruct, nourish, and refresh the pilgrims before the final leg of their journey. The Shining Ones are radiant beings who live in the Celestial Country and who periodically visit Beulah, which borders it, to welcome newly arrived pilgrims.

The Lord of the Way, the Hill, and the Celestial City

The true central character of the story is the Lord of the Way, or Christ, whose presence is mostly felt through the provisions he makes for his pilgrims along the path. Although we never see him under that name, he appears in various guises (or so it seems), such as the Keeper of the Wicket Gate, the Interpreter, the Good Shepherd, and the King of the Celestial City, and he is also spoken of as the Lord of the Hill.

Book Summary

Opening Apology

The use of allegory—The first few pages of John Bunyan's *The Pilgrim's Progress,* called "the author's apology," are in poem form. He begins by relating how, as he set out to write another book about the Christian path, he suddenly found himself writing the allegory that evolved into *The Pilgrim's Progress.* The fact that the book is in allegorical form is significant for two reasons: Bunyan intended to transmit the story as a dream, and that intention, in turn, was fueled by the desire to communicate the notion that this life—the material existence that seems so real and substantial—is nothing more than an illusion.

The decision to publish—There seems to have been some dissension among those exposed to Bunyan's initial attempts at writing *The Pilgrim's Progress* as to whether he should publish it. According to his poetic apology, he finally decided to go ahead with it to please those in favor and because those opposed would not be hurt by what they could choose to avoid. Furthermore, he reasoned, one should not judge something by its immediate appearance. The analogy he uses is rain clouds, which seem unattractive by their dark appearance, yet have the advantage that they bring rain; whereas bright clouds might look appealing but are unable to nourish the earth. He takes the analogy one step further by saying that when the earth is in need of nourishment, it is grateful for what it receives from either source, dark or bright. He seems to be saying that the same is true of men: those in search of spiritual nourishment are grateful for it when it appears in any form, while the more worldly-minded are prone to judge by externals.

Arguments for allegory—Next he takes the opposite approach by drawing the analogy to the fisherman and the fowler, who use every means they can devise to catch their fish or their birds, though they still fail in some instances. For those, they need a special technique to lure them in—a reference to the possible advantage of using allegory instead of direct argument to make his point. He then returns to his previous reasoning that a thing should never be judged by its outward appearance—that precious gems can be found in unexpected places, and that even Jesus hid powerful spiritual truths in obscure parables. Yet those who are accustomed to reading those parables would never dare to criticize them as an invalid mode of communicating momentous truths.

Further justifications for using allegory—This last point and others indicate that Bunyan felt largely criticized by men who considered themselves religious—not surprisingly, since his unorthodox views were what landed him in jail. In fact, he addresses the "man of god" (the conservatively religious person) directly on three issues:

1. The wording is a little obscure, but Bunyan seems to be saying that he is justified in using allegory because he does not abuse it but uses it to convey Truth. He also repeats his previous point that others of a more exalted nature and spiritual position (presumably Jesus, the prophets, and apostles) also used allegory.

2. His second argument is similar: he brings up the point that some people use dialogue as a means of conveying Truth, and no one criticizes them for it. He adds in his defense that if it pleases God to guide his writing in that direction, then who are we to judge?
3. Point 3 reiterates the fact that scripture favors allegory in many cases, and he feels himself, therefore, justified in using it as a technique.

The purpose of the book—Bunyan finishes his points by committing the work to God. But before embarking on the project, he describes the book's basic purpose:

- to give an account of its main character (the seeker after spiritual salvation) and the path he takes
- to describe the paths of those who start out well but end as fools
- to give direction to those who are ready to accept it
- to galvanize the slothful, open the eyes of the blind, and comfort the helpless—in short, to awaken us from the dream we call life

Part I

The dream—The story begins with a clear statement that what we are about to experience is a dream. The narrator's first act is to lie down and go to sleep, and it's then that the story begins. The significance, as emphasized in the introduction, is that our worldly, material life is a dream, and that only as we awaken to the Divine Life do we begin to experience reality. Until then, we are thoroughly steeped in the dream, which we mistake for reality.

Christian's awakening to his desperate state and the need to escape—The first event in this dream world is the narrator's encounter with the main character, a man dressed in rags, carrying a heavy burden, and reading a book that causes him to tremble and weep in despair. Once home, he (who so far has no name) can no longer contain himself as he explains to his wife and children that their city is destined to be destroyed with fire from heaven unless they can find a means of escape. His family, convinced that he is feverish, sends him to bed, thinking that some sleep will do him good. By morning, however, he is in even worse shape, whereupon his family tries harsher means to bring him around, but with no luck. He, in turn, resorts to prayer and solitude, having received no support from his family.

Evangelist directs Christian to the Wicket Gate—
When the narrator encounters him, he is reading the book that he usually has with him and wondering out loud how he can be saved. As he looks around trying to figure out his next move, the character called Evangelist enters and asks him why he is crying. The man answers that he has learned, to his dismay, that he is destined to die and be judged, neither of which are appealing, especially since he fears that the burden he carries will sink him to hell. Ascertaining that he needs direction, Evangelist hands him a parchment scroll that says, "Fly from the Wrath to come." When the man asks him where he needs to go, Evangelist points toward a Wicket Gate, which the man cannot see, and a Shining Light, which he sees only faintly. He decides, however, to trust Evangelist's guidance and runs toward the Light, believing that it will show him the way to eternal Life.

Obstinate and Pliable try to detain Christian—His family and neighbors try to detain him with their cries, mockery, and threats, but without success. Two of them, Obstinate and Pliable, actually follow and eventually catch up with him. They try to persuade him to return with them, but he refuses, telling them that what he seeks is of a higher, incorruptible nature than the regular comforts and companionship. Obstinate, convinced that the man—whose name we now learn is Christian—is out of his mind, decides that it's a hopeless case and that he and Pliable should let him go his way while they return. Pliable, however, is receptive to Christian's advice and wants to go with him. Obstinate tries to dissuade him, though unsuccessfully, and convinced that they're both delusional, he returns alone.

Pliable joins Christian on his pilgrimage to the new world—Now on their own, Pliable and Christian discuss the new and better world to which they are headed. Christian emphasizes that it is difficult to describe in regular terms. Its characteristics include, for example, infinity, immortality, transcendent radiance, and pure bliss. Its people are holy, loving, and harmless, every one of them attuned to the ways of God—and there are many to have preceded them on the path, some of whom have suffered terribly but who are now well and whole.

The Slough of Despond and Pliable's desertion—
Excited, Pliable suggests they pick up the pace, but Christian informs him that the burden he bears forces him to go more slowly than he would like. At that point, they both accidentally step into the Slough of Despond, a symbol of depression and despair, where they become stuck in the mire. Angry and feeling betrayed, Pliable asks Christian to explain himself, which he can't. Pliable then decides that he's had enough, struggles to free himself, and returns home, leaving Christian by himself.

Help arrives for Christian—Undeterred, Christian aims to reach the side of the Slough nearest the Wicket Gate. Saddled with his burden, he struggles with enormous difficulty to free himself from the bog, when a stranger named Help appears and offers him a hand. Having pointed him in the right direction and brought him up onto solid land, Help sends Christian on his way.

The Slough and its difficulties—At this juncture in the story, the narrator steps in (in a rare appearance) to question Help about the existence of the Slough of Despond and why it hasn't been fixed. Help explains to him that a great deal of effort has been put into trying to fix it but that the burden of sin has made it difficult. He explains that often, when a person starts on the path, fear and doubt arise in his heart and make the going difficult. For those who are careful to look, there are definite and beneficial steps placed throughout the Slough that will lead the seeker out until he reaches the Gate and is on solid ground again. However, the extent of the filth in the Slough is such that many perfectly miss the steps.

Pliable's return and reception—Once home, Pliable has to put up with the ridicule of his neighbors, though some support his choice to return, calling it wise. Ashamed at first, he keeps to himself, but once his confidence improves, he joins with the others in criticizing Christian.

Mr. Worldly Wiseman directs Christian to the town of Morality—Now alone, Christian soon meets with another person coming toward him from the other direction. That person is Mr. Worldly Wiseman, from the city of Carnal Policy, near Christian's hometown of Destruction. Mr. Worldly Wiseman recognizes Christian from the descriptions he has heard, since there was a lot of gossip about him when he first set out. Addressing him as an inferior because of his relative social status, he questions him about his journey, his family, and his burden and then seeks to give him advice about his quest. He tries to deter Christian from pursuing his path, which he describes as a perilous journey, fraught with nothing but troubles, including hunger, fatigue, pain, darkness—even death. Christian protests that his burden is worse than all those troubles put together and that since this path promises deliverance from this horrible burden, he is willing to take it. Mr. Worldly Wiseman asks Christian how he obtained his burden, to which the latter replies that it was the result of reading the book he was carrying. Unsurprised, Mr. Worldly Wiseman claims that the book has been guilty of causing such situations before by introducing people to ideas that are beyond their reach and that send them on fruitless quests. He recommends a different path, a better, safer way that is guaranteed to bring happiness and friendship. Evidently weary from his travels, Christian asks him for his secret. Mr. Worldly Wiseman replies that there is a man named Legality in the nearby village of Morality, whose skill at easing other men's burdens is well known. If Legality happens to not be home, his son Civility can take his place. Furthermore, should Christian desire to live in the town of Morality, he will find for himself and his family many vacant houses, ample provisions, and decent neighbors such as Credit (credibility) and Good Fashion.

Christian's fear of the steep, flaming hill—Eager to shed his burden, Christian asks Mr. Worldly Wiseman to show him the way and is directed toward a high hill. But as he nears the hill, it seems overwhelmingly steep to him, and with his burden feeling heavier than ever, he finds himself at a standstill, with serious concerns that the hill might fall on him and crush him. Even worse, it was emitting flames that threatened to burn him.

Evangelist directs Christian back to the Way—As he stands there regretting that he has taken Mr. Worldly Wiseman's advice and turned aside from the Way, Evangelist appears, looking extremely displeased. Approaching nearer, he begins to question Christian about what he is doing there and why he has turned aside from his original instructions. Christian then describes his encounter with Mr. Worldly Wiseman and how the promise to be rid of his burden inspired him to follow his instructions. Evangelist then explains to Christian exactly who Mr. Worldly Wiseman is and why Christian should avoid his advice at all costs. He specifies that there are three aspects of his advice that he must learn to hate. These are:

1. his turning him from the Way of Christ

2. his attempts to make him hate the Cross

3. his advice to take a path that can lead only to Death

The Wicket Gate as the only entrance to the Way and Life—He reminds Christian that the true Way leads to a narrow Gate and that only through that Gate can one attain Life. All other ways lead to death and must be avoided. Furthermore, those who would tread this Way must make it their only priority. The nature of the Cross is to sacrifice everything else to attain Life eternal, so any doctrines that try to persuade him to do otherwise must be avoided. Finally, he emphasizes that all paths leading away from the Way can only lead to death and cannot remove his burden, even though the promise to do so. He explains that Mr. Legality and his son Civility are the offspring of the Bondwoman and are, therefore, incapable of freeing anyone, since they are themselves under the curse of the Law.

Ashamed, Christian asks whether there is any hope for him to still be accepted at the Gate. Evangelist says that though his sin is grievous, the man at the gate possesses goodwill toward all and will, therefore, allow him in. He then encourages him with a smile and a kiss and sends him on his way with the warning to avoid forbidden pathways and to stay on the recommended Way.

Christian's renewed focus and determination— This time, Christian is determined to take Evangelist's advice and not to digress again. As he makes his way back to the path, he maintains his focus and avoids all conversation with passersby. At last, he comes to the Wicket Gate, which reads, "Knock, and it shall be opened unto you." Following instructions, he knocks several times, until the gate is finally opened by a serious-looking individual. It is Goodwill himself, who asks him his name, his origin, and his business, and having established that his purpose is true, he pulls Christian through the Gate to avoid the arrows that are shot from Beelzebub's nearby castle.

The meeting with Goodwill, the Keeper of the Gate—Once Christian is through the Gate, Goodwill asks him a few more questions about how he learned of the Gate's whereabouts and the details of his journey—why he was alone, his neighbors' reactions, Pliable's discouragement, his meeting with Mr. Worldly Wiseman, his trepidation at the foot of the mountain, and the grace he experienced through Evangelist's setting him straight again. Christian's gratitude for being let through the gate is met with Goodwill's reassurance that none who come are rejected, no matter what they might have done previously. He then instructs him to come with him to learn further about the straight and narrow Way. Christian asks Goodwill whether he can help him to remove his burden, but Goodwill tells him to be patient and that it will fall off by itself once he reaches the place of Deliverance. Goodwill then instructs him to watch for the Interpreter's house and to knock once he arrives, as the Interpreter will teach him important things. After that, he sends Christian on his way.

The Interpreter's house and the true Guide—
Following Goodwill's instructions, Christian arrives at the door of the Interpreter's house and knocks. After the usual questions, he is led to the Interpreter, who shows him into a private room. There on the wall is the picture of an extremely serious person, who is clearly a man of God in the service of spiritual Truth. His gaze is turned toward Heaven, he holds the Bible in his hand, a golden Crown stands above his head, and the World is behind him. The Interpreter's purpose in showing Christian the picture is to introduce him to his true Guide. All others are false and should be distrusted and avoided, since the paths to which they lead all end in death.

The parlor full of dust—Next the Interpreter leads Christian into a large parlor full of dust. The Interpreter summons a man to sweep it, but the dust is so plentiful that it only makes things worse. To solve the problem, a Damsel sprinkles water around the parlor so that it can be cleaned with ease. When Christian asks what the scene means, the Interpreter explains that the parlor is the heart; the dust is the sin that has defiled man's soul; the man sweeping is the Law; and the young lady sprinkling water is the Grace that proceeds from the Gospel.

The two boys, Passion and Patience—After that, the Interpreter takes Christian into another room with two young boys named Passion and Patience. Christian observes that Passion is restless and unhappy because he doesn't want to wait for the good he has been promised, while Patience sits quietly. Moreover, when Passion is presented with a bag of treasure, he first scorns Patience for having nothing, then quickly squanders what he has until only rags remain. Christian learns that Passion represents the men and the things of this world, while Patience represents those of the next. They are equated with the story of Dives and Lazarus, the rich man and the beggar who exchanged places in the next life, much to the dismay of the former. The principle they represent is that the first shall be last, and the last shall be first, and the Interpreter further reminds Christian that the things of this world are mere shadows compared to the eternal Glory of the world to come.

The fire and the oil, or the work of Grace—Next, the Interpreter leads him to a wall with a fire burning against it. A man keeps throwing water onto the fire in an effort to put it out, but his efforts have the opposite effect. Then the Interpreter leads Christian around to the other side of the wall, where another man, unseen to the first, stands with a vessel of oil, from which he repeatedly feeds the fire. The Interpreter explains that the fire stands for the effect of Grace, which the Devil tries to extinguish but which only burns more strongly as Christ secretly feeds the flames with the oil of Grace.

The man who breaks down the Palace door—Following that, Christian is led to a lovely place with a beautiful Palace, with people dressed in gold walking on the rooftop. Numerous people are standing at the door, wanting to go in, but they are blocked by armed guards. Seated at a table near the door, there is a man with a book and an inkwell, whose task is to write down the names of those allowed to enter. Most of the group is deterred by the armed men, but one especially confident man walks up to the scribe, tells him to write his name in the book, and after arming himself, rushes at the guards. After a fierce fight, he manages to hack his way through the guards and into the Palace. At that point, a pleasing voice is heard welcoming him and promising him eternal Glory, upon which he enters and his dressed in garments of gold. Excited and pleased, Christian asks to go up to the Palace but is told to wait until he has seen a few more things.

The man in the Iron Cage—Next, the Interpreter brings Christian to a dark room where he shows him a man in an Iron Cage, who is heavy with sadness. On asking about his plight and how he got there, the man tells Christian that he has shut himself into a cage of despair through his carelessness. Because he turned away from the things of the Spirit and instead gave himself over to the things of this world, he now is no longer allowed to repent and is permanently barred from the Grace of God. The Interpreter admonishes Christian to remember this example and then takes him to the next scene.

The fearful dream of Judgment Day—Finally, the Interpreter brings Christian to a room where they see a man getting out of bed and dressing himself. The man appears to be in a great state of fear, and when asked about it, he explains that he had a dream of Judgment Day, in which he saw himself as one of the rejected sinners, the chaff that is gathered up and burned. He was also tormented by his own conscience and had the fearful opportunity to look down into the gaping mouth of hell. When he saw others being taken up to Heaven and found himself left behind, he concluded that he was not ready for Judgment Day.

The Interpreter's final words of advice—Now done with the lessons, the Interpreter asks Christian whether he has thought about everything he has seen. Christian answers that he has and that the scenes make him both hopeful and fearful. The Interpreter urges him to keep them in mind as he goes on his journey, and he encourages him with the knowledge that the Comforter will accompany and guide him along the Way.

Christian loses his burden by the Cross and the Sepulchre—Finally, Christian sets out on his way again, which the narrator describes as a highway fenced in on both sides with the Wall of Salvation. At this point, Christian is running, though still with a heavy load on this back. Eventually, he comes to a place where the road begins to go upward. That place is marked by a Cross, and below, at the base of the hill, is a Sepulchre. As Christian arrives at the Cross, his burden suddenly unhinges, falls off, rolls down the hill into the Sepulchre and is never seen again.

The Shining Ones and the scroll—Christian now feels light and cheerful but also deeply moved by the sight of the Cross that has taken away his burden, and he begins to weep. As he stands there weeping, he is approached by three radiant beings of light, described as Shining Ones, each of whom performs a different function. The first forgives his sins; the second clothes him in a new garment; and the third puts a mark on his forehead and furnishes him with a scroll, which he is to read along the Way and hand in when he reaches the Celestial Gate. After that, they depart, and Christian, joyfully leaping and singing, continues on his way.

Simple, Sloth, and Presumption—His next stop is at the base of the hill, where he spies three sleeping men off to the side, with their heels chained. Seeing that they are in danger, he turns aside to warn them, offering also to help remove their chains. The first man, whose name is Simple, says that he sees no danger. The second, named Sloth, prefers to sleep a little more. And the third, called Presumption, insists that self-reliance is the best path. With that, they go back to sleep.

Formalist and Hypocrisy—Christian has no choice but to move on, but their inability to see the truth of his warning and the value of his offer bothers him. Suddenly, two men leap over the wall on the left-hand side and hurry up to him. They introduce themselves as Formalist and Hypocrisy, both from the land of Vain-Glory and on their way to Mount Zion. When he questions them as to why they leapt over the Wall instead of coming in by the Gate, they claim that the Gate is too far out of their pathway and that they prefer to take a shortcut. When Christian protests that such an approach will be counted as thievery, they cite their thousand-year-old custom. Surely, they reason, it will hold up when submitted to trial. But Christian is not convinced, though they insist that the fact that they have made it onto the Way is good enough and that how they got there should make no difference. He counters that it is important to walk by the rule of the Lord of the Way and that not to do so will backfire on them and ultimately have them ousted. Still not convinced, they insist that they practice the Laws and Ordinances as well as he does, but he replies that Laws and Ordinances cannot save them. They insist that he is no better than they are and that the only difference is that coat that he wears, which hides his nakedness. With that, he tells them who gave him the coat and also that they put a mark on his forehead and gave him a scroll, to be handed in upon reaching the Celestial City. Ignorant as ever, they pay no heed to him, instead laughing at him. From that point onward, Christian keeps to himself, reading from his scroll as he goes.

The Hill Difficulty and the two false paths—
Eventually, the three travelers come to the Hill Difficulty. At this point, the path split three ways. The one that continues from the Way that leads from the Wicket Gate is also called Difficulty, and it is clear that it leads right up the hill, which is steep. The other two seem like they might be easier, though they are named Danger and Destruction. Having decided not to deviate from the original path, Christian chooses the way called Difficulty without hesitation. The two other travelers prefer the other roads, having convinced themselves that they will end up in the same place as Christian. But the path called Danger leads to a forest, and the path called Destruction delivers as promised: the person who chose it fell to his death in a field surrounded by dark mountains.

Falling asleep in the Arbor—Christian, meanwhile, continues climbing steadily up the hill. He had slowed to a walk and then a crawl because the hill was so steep, until he came to an Arbor, where he paused to refresh himself. As he sits reading his scroll and admiring his coat, he falls asleep. He is awakened by someone reciting the Proverb, "Go to the ant, thou sluggard," which causes him to jump up and continue hastily to the top of the hill.

Mistrust and Timorous—Once at the top of the hill, Christian encounters Mistrust and Timorous, who had been on their way to Zion but now turned back because they had spotted some lions and were in doubt as to their own safety and survival. Afraid, Christian nevertheless reasons that it is better to go forward than back, since to go back is certain destruction, whereas to go forward brings at least a promise of life. Desirous of comfort, he reaches for his scroll, only to find that it is not there. Distraught, he tries to think of what might have happened to it and then remembers that he fell asleep in the Arbor. He resolves to make his way back to find it, since it is his only guarantee of entrance into the Celestial City and since it has brought him much comfort along the Way. He chides himself for having fallen asleep in the Arbor, especially since the Lord of the Hill intended it only for a short pause, but eventually he finds his way back and discovers the scroll underneath a bench.

The chained lions—He joyfully thanks God for his mercy and hurries back up the hill, especially since night is falling fast. This renews his fear as he realizes that he still has to pass the lions, which are more likely to prowl for their prey at night. Still, he continues on his way, when suddenly a beautiful Castle looms before him. Hopeful at the prospect of staying there for the night, he hurries toward it, when he sees a narrow passage leading there and, in the passage, the two lions he heard of earlier. As he is contemplating returning, the Porter, whose name is Watchful, shouts at him to not be afraid, that the lions are chained and can do no harm. They have been placed there as a test of faith, and if Christian stays in the middle of the path, he will be safe.

The Porter at the Castle Gate—Following the Porter's instructions, Christian makes it safely to the gate of the Castle. Inquiring whether he may stay there for the night, he discovers that the Castle was built by the Lord of the Hill to give safety and rest to the true pilgrims along the Way. The Porter asks him his name and why he has arrived so late. Christian tells him his story, and the Porter replies that he will call one of the maidens of the household, who will interview him further before deciding what to do.

The maidens Discretion, Prudence, Piety, and Charity—When the maiden, whose name is Discretion, arrives, she also asks Christian the usual questions about his origin, his purpose, and his name. She then calls three more maidens, all virgins named Prudence, Piety, and Charity, who question him some more and finally admit him into the Castle, which is called the House Beautiful. While dinner is being prepared, Prudence, Piety, and Charity, continue their conversation with Christian. They question him about whether he ever thought about his former country, how he had been directed onto the Way, and what he had seen so far. They also ask how he overcame his inner challenges, whether he was married with children, and why his family had stayed behind.

Rest and refreshment for body and soul—Supper was spent discussing the greatness and goodness of their Lord—his power over death, his great heart for the poor, and the extraordinary sacrifice he made for their benefit and elevation. When dinner was ended, having prayed for protection, they took Christian to his room, called Peace, and they all went to bed.

The maidens of the Castle teach Christian—The next day, they brought him to the Study, where they read from the Records about their Lord's heritage as the Son of God, his many impressive acts, the acts of his servants, and his generosity and openness toward all who came to him.

The Armory—On the following day, they took Christian to the castle's Armory, which housed much weaponry and armor for the benefit of the Lord's pilgrims, in addition to historical weapons and tools used in times past by famous servants such as Samson, David, Gideon, and Moses.

The view of the Delectable Mountains—On Christian's last day there, the maidens brought him to the roof of the Castle, where they told him to look to the South. There, he saw the Delectable Mountains, a beautiful country of forests, springs, fruit, flowers, and vineyards. The country was called Emmanuel's Land (meaning the Land of God's Presence), and from there, he would be shown the Gate of the Celestial City.

Continuing the journey: the steep descent to the Valley of Humiliation—Finally, they let him part, as he had been eager to do, but not without first thoroughly outfitting him with gear from the Armory. As Christian was leaving, he asked Watchful, the Porter, whether he had seen any other pilgrims, to which Watchful replied that he had seen one named Faithful, who happened to be a friend of Christian's from his former hometown. When Christian asked how far he might have gone by now, the Porter replied that he was probably already past the base of the Hill. As Christian bade the Porter farewell with blessings and thanks, the four maidens accompanied him down the Hill to the Valley of Humiliation. Christian had already perceived that it would be as difficult to go down as it had been to climb up, which the three maidens confirmed. Having reached the bottom, they gave him provisions—wine, bread, and raisins—and then parted ways.

The battle with the demon Apollyon—No sooner had Christian entered the Valley of Humiliation than he was approached by a demon named Apollyon, or "Destroyer," who was the lord of Christian's previous hometown, Destruction. Consequently, he felt that he owned Christian and, therefore, set about to dissuade him from following the Way and serving his new Lord. But Christian was fearful of eternal destruction and furthermore determined to be true to his word to serve his new Master, whom he loved and whose ways, people, and places were much more to his liking. After a prolonged argument with Christian, the demon—who had the wings of a dragon and the scales of a fish—flew into a rage, so great was his hatred of the Lord of the Hill. Christian and Apollyon then entered into a fierce battle that lasted more than half a day and did much damage to both sides. In fact, when Christian was near the end of his strength and had lost his sword in a fall, it seemed that he was almost done, when at the last moment, just as Apollyon was about to destroy him, Christian managed to regain his sword and deal him a powerful, near-fatal blow. With that, the demon, who had been roaring and shouting the whole time, spread his wings and was gone from sight. For the first time during the entire fight, Christian raised his eyes upward and smiled. He then said a prayer of thanks to his deliverer. As he was finishing, a hand appeared with leaves from the Tree of Life that instantly healed his wounds. Following that, he nourished himself with some of his provisions and then set out on his journey, this time with his sword in hand.

The Valley of the Shadow of Death—As Christian ventured forth, he came to another, even more desolate valley, the Valley of the Shadow of the Death. Upon nearing it, he was met by two men coming back from that direction, who warned him not to go in. They themselves had not entered it but had seen it, and they described it as being pitch black, with a pit full of goblins, dragons, and satyrs. Moreover, they had heard horrible howling noises emerging from the pit, and the feeling they sensed was one of death and confusion. But Christian knew from their description that he had to go this way to reach the Celestial City and be truly safe. And so he continued, alone and undaunted, but still on his guard against possible danger.

The frightening sounds and sensations of the Valley—The way through the Valley was indeed treacherous, with a ditch on one side and a quagmire on the other. The path was extremely narrow and so dark that it was impossible to see even one step ahead. The ditch was a common trap for the blind leading the blind, and the quagmire was so deep that there was no place for a person to rest his feet. Even worse, in the middle of the Valley, right near the path, Hell opened wide its gaping mouth. The tremendous quantity of smoke and fire and the horrendous sounds that emerged from that pit were so incompatible with Christian's sword that he had to put it away for the time being and instead resort entirely to prayer as his means of strength and protection. Many times, he felt he was in grave danger, being surrounded by flames and howling and gusting energies, all of which threatened him. At one point, as he was accosted by a group of fiends, he cried out in the name of God, and the fiends backed away. Most disturbing, though, was the fiend who, unbeknownst to Christian, whispered blasphemous thoughts in his ear so that he had difficulty telling which thoughts were his own, and this left him wondering why he was thinking blasphemies at all.

After a long while, it seemed to him that he heard the voice of another pilgrim reciting Psalm 23:

"Though I walk through the Valley

of the Shadow of Death,

I will fear no evil, for thou art with me."

This was a massive comfort to Christian, since it meant that God must be present and that there was another believer nearby. He hoped that they might meet and keep each other company along the Way.

Sunrise over the Valley of the Shadow of Death— As the sun rose over the Valley, Christian looked back to see where he had been. He could now clearly view the narrowness of the path, with the ditch and the quagmire on either side and the dragons, hobgoblins, and satyrs in the pit. He could also see that the part of the Valley that still lay ahead was even more daunting, full of pitfalls and traps of different kinds, and he was grateful for the light.

The cave of the giants Pope and Pagan—Toward the end of the Valley, Christian found himself walking amidst the remains of dead pilgrims who had gone before him. They had been murdered by the giants who from ancient times lived in a nearby cave. One of the giants, Pagan, had long since died, and the other, Pope, had grown so old and rigid that he had been rendered harmless. And so, Christian was able to make his way safely past the cave.

Christian meets Faithful—Soon after that, Christian arrived at a little hill, and seeing Faithful ahead of him, he ran to meet him and overtook him. In a moment of pride at now being first, he forgot to watch where he was going and fell. Fortunately, he was able to get up with Faithful's help, and after that, they walked together in a spirit of love. As they walked, Faithful told him how he had stayed in the city of Destruction for as long as possible but then finally left, knowing that it would be destroyed. He said that the neighbors had talked a great deal about its destruction but seemed not to actually believe that it would happen. He also told Christian of Pliable's unfortunate fate—that no one took him seriously anymore and that he couldn't even get a job. Even worse, he seemed so ashamed that he avoided speaking to Faithful, though Faithful himself would have been willing.

Faithful's experiences on his journey—Christian then asked Faithful about his own adventures along the Way. Faithful told him that he had managed to avoid the Slough of Despond but had instead encountered a woman named Wanton, who had tried to seduce him and maligned him when she failed to do so. On arriving at the foot of the Hill Difficulty, he was met by an old man, who called himself Adam the first (Christ being the second Adam, according to St. Paul). Adam the first came from the town of Deceit, and his goal was to ensnare Faithful with promises of the good things of this world in return for lifelong servitude (though he called it "inheritance"). But Faithful noticed a warning written on the old man's head that read: "Put off the Old Man with his Deeds." Perceiving that he would end up as a slave rather than an heir, Faithful rejected his offer, upon which the old man threatened and abused him, both verbally and even physically by tugging violently at his flesh. Faithful, however, got away and continued climbing the Hill of Difficulty. Just as Faithful reached the Arbor, he noticed a man running after him until he finally caught up with him by the bench. Three times he knocked Faithful down, dealing him a near-fatal blow each time. But as he was about to finish him off, a man with holes in his hands and side appeared and told him to refrain. Seeing the holes, Faithful recognized him as the Lord of the Hill, after which he continued his pilgrimage.

Christian explained to Faithful that the man who kept knocking him down was Moses, the representative of the Law. That was why he showed no mercy—because he was the representative of justice. Christian then asked Faithful whether he hadn't noticed the great House that was guarded by the Porter. Faithful said that he saw both the House and the Lions, who luckily were asleep, since it was midday. But because he had so much of the day still ahead of him, he chose to continue down the Hill.

Faithful's journey through the Valley of Humiliation—Next, Christian asked Faithful whether he had met anyone on his way through the Valley of Humiliation. Faithful responded that he had met someone named Discontent, who tried to persuade him that to walk through the Valley would be lacking in honor because it went against all worldly notions of glory and achievement. Faithful would be a traitor to his friends, he claimed, but Faithful noted that these former friends—Pride, Arrogance, Worldly Success, and Vanity—had deserted him when he set out on his pilgrimage. He also no longer had any need of them, especially since he had grasped the value of humility and the danger of pride.

The meeting with Shame—Christian then asked him whether he had met anyone else there, to which Faithfulness replied that he met someone called Shame but that his name did not match his behavior. Shame, so-called, was bold-faced and negatively disposed toward religion, which he felt impinged too much on men's liberties, preventing them from acting freely and boldly (in the bullying sense) and instead making them overly conscientious. Those who succeeded in the world had no use for such things and counted pilgrims as foolish and ignorant. Considering religious notions to be shameful and wasteful, he esteemed the virtuous to be useless, and the base to be great. Faithful, however, understood that this was the reverse of the truth, and after a mighty effort, he was finally able to fight off Shame and his demands to forsake the Way. Christian applauded Faithful for his perceptiveness and steadfastness, adding that Shame's bold statements are opposed to the good and in favor of foolishness. Faithful added that it is important to block Shame's attempts to steer them away from the path of Truth.

When asked whether he had had any further encounters, Faithful said that he had not, since the remainder of his travels were by daylight, including through the Valley of the Shadow of Death. Christian then told him of his own encounter with Apollyon, who nearly destroyed him, but with the grace of God, he escaped and continued on his way out of the Valley of Humiliation and through the Valley of the Shadow of Death.

Talkative and his hypocritical chatter—At this point in the journey, Faithful and Christian meet another traveler named Talkative, who claims to be a pilgrim on his way to Heaven. When asked by Faithful whether he wants to join them, he willingly accepts. They quickly discover that he likes nothing more than to talk about heavenly ideas, but though he claims to link his talk to profitable action, in actuality, he seems more interested in endless conceptualization. When Faithful privately asks Christian of his opinion of Talkative, Christian reveals that he knows him from their former hometown. His father's name is Prating-Row, known for his chatter; and though Talkative's conversation seems impressive at first, on closer inspection, both he and his words lose their charm. At first amused by Faithful's naïveté, Christian then grows more serious, explaining that Talkative's religion has no basis in his life or heart but is entirely focused on his speech, which is the same no matter where he is or with whom or in what state—whether sober or drunk. He reminds Faithful of the saying that "the Kingdom of God is not in word, but in power," and that although Talkative might chatter endlessly about the elements of true religion, he does little to back up this talk. Christian knows this for a fact, having seen Talkative at home, where he realized that there was no evidence of genuine, heartfelt religion. The common folk who knew him well, including his servants, said the same thing—that his behavior was fraudulent, hypocritical, and cruel. Even the way he raises his sons is the opposite of true religion, and Christian concludes that such behavior does more damage than good.

The importance of words backed by deeds—
Having listened intently to Christian's descriptions of Talkative, Faithful concludes that he was deceived, and resolves to be more careful from now on in his observations of any discrepancies between words and deeds. He bases his conclusion on Christian's overall character and the fact that he would not lightly make statements of this sort. Christian confirms his observations with the claim that good men who know Talkative well feel shame at the mere mention of his name. In response to Faithful's recognition that true religion requires more than just talk, Christian likens it to the harvest, which is judged by the abundance of its fruits. He compares talking to the sowing of seed, which must grow into a way of life if it is to be judged as bearing fruit. Faithful then makes the further comparison with Moses' definition of clean versus unclean beasts. To be clean, an animal must both part the hoof and chew the cud. Talkative only chews the cud; that is, he might think and talk about the meaning of various scriptural concepts, but he does not make the necessary life changes to prove his sincerity. Christian adds that he lacks the sense of grace that fulfills the law and makes his talk, in the words of St. Paul, more than "sounding brass."

Faithful confronts Talkative—Once Faithful is convinced that Christian speaks the truth about Talkative, the next question in his mind is how to get away from his baneful company. To that end, Christian has a plan, which, if Faithful follows it, should either convert Talkative's heart or drive him away. The idea is to begin by doing what Talkative loves best—to talk about religion—but to then tie it to the realities of the heart, the home, and everyday life. This Faithful does, even taking it one step farther by asking Talkative point blank whether he applies the ideas to his daily life. The topic they broach is how the heart experiences the presence of Divine Grace, both at first and later. Talkative answers that it first cries out against sin and, later, that it gains knowledge of the Divine mysteries. In both cases, Faithful tries to point out the possibility of hypocrisy and the need to connect the ideas to a genuine Christian life. Talkative, now slightly uncomfortable, accuses him of trying to snare him. Faithful insists that he is only trying to make things right. Ultimately, however, he tells him up front that he has heard bad things about his lifestyle, especially in comparison with his words. Eventually, Talkative, who is now finding the conversation too judgmental, excuses himself and leaves. Christian's plan has worked, and he and Faithful are now free to move on without him. Faithful, for his part, is glad that he was straightforward with Talkative, and his hope is that some day their conversation will come to Talkative's remembrance in a helpful way—but if not, then at least Faithful's conscience can rest at ease.

The final meeting with Evangelist and the prophecy of death at Vanity Fair—As Faithful and Christian neared the end of the wilderness, they spotted Evangelist coming toward them. They greeted each other with gladness, after which Evangelist asked them how they were doing, what sorts of encounters they had had along the Way, and how they had reacted. The two pilgrims told him about their various encounters and then listened as he encouraged and warned them about some pitfalls to expect on the path. Knowing of his wisdom and his ability to see the future, Christian and Faithful asked Evangelist to speak further. He then warned them of their impending deaths in the town they would enter after leaving the wilderness, but he counseled them to be firm in their faith, for by doing so, they would receive the Crown of Life. They should therefore view their troubles as an escape from suffering that others with a longer sojourn on earth would have to endure.

The town of Vanity and Vanity Fair—And so, as the pilgrims came to the end of the wilderness, they entered a town called Vanity, the site of an ancient and renowned fair known as Vanity Fair. This fair sold all manner of goods from all over the world, including various honors and relationships—anything pertaining to material or worldly experience. Anyone going to the Celestial City had to go through this town, with the exception of those who chose to exit the world completely. Even Christ passed through on his way there and was tempted by the Lord of the Fair (the Prince of this World) the whole time. The pilgrims, therefore, were no exception, and because they were noticeably different from the people of that town, they caused quite a stir. Not only were they dressed differently, but they also spoke a different language, and most of all, they showed little interest in the merchandise. They did not hide the fact that their goal was Heaven and their focus Ultimate Truth.

Abuse and imprisonment of the pilgrims by the townsfolk—At first, the townsfolk figured they were fools or madmen, but when the pilgrims rejected their wares, their attitudes quickly turned to contempt and even physical abuse. Finally, they called the Lord of the Fair, who had the pilgrims questioned. Those who questioned them did not believe them, concluded that they were mad, and subjected them to beatings, humiliation, and imprisonment in a cage, where they became the objects of further mockery and abuse.

Conflict over the pilgrims results in further abuse—Some of the townspeople were more reasonable and objected to the treatment the pilgrims received. That led to a fight between the two sides, which in turn led to additional accusation and punishment of the two pilgrims. But the pilgrims' behavior through it all was so wise and compliant that a few of the townsfolk sided with them, but that led only to even more humiliation and abuse, including threats of death.

The pilgrims' trial and Faithful's defense—Finally, after continued imprisonment, the two pilgrims were brought to trial before the judge, Lord Hate-Good. There they suffered all the usual untrue accusations: that they had interfered with commerce and caused a disturbance of the peace, and furthermore, that they had convinced others to do so. Then Faithful stated that they had behaved peacefully, that their innocence and honesty had won over some of the townsfolk and that his only protest was against the Lord of the Fair for pitting himself against the Most High.

Accusation of Faithful by Envy, Superstition, and Pickthank—At that point, three witnesses came forward: Envy, Superstition, and Pickthank. Envy, who was the first to take the stand, accused Faithful of claiming that Christianity and the laws of Vanity contradicted each other and that Faithful had tried his best to win people over to the former. Next, Superstition took the stand and related Faithful's opinion that the town's religious practices were, like its name, pure vanity. Finally, Pickthank, accused Faithful of slandering the nobility of the town of Vanity, including the Lords Old-Man, Luxurious, Carnal Delight, Desire of Vain-Glory, Lechery, Having Greedy, Judge Hate-Good himself, and even the Prince of the town, Beelzebub.

Faithful's final self-defense in the name of good—Once the witnesses were done, Faithful asked to speak on his own behalf, which he was grudgingly granted. First, he stated that he was only opposed to whatever opposed the Word of God; second, that whatever did not proceed from Divine Faith and Revelation was wasted effort in relation to the attainment of eternal Life; and third, that though he did not see himself as "railing" upon anyone, he agreed that the Lord of the town and all his attendant lords belonged in Hell. Having concluded his statements, he commended himself to God.

The verdict of the Court of vice, Faithful's cruel execution, and his ascent into Heaven—After he was done, Lord Hate-Good, the judge, instructed the jury in the history of their law. He told them of the deeds of three servants of the Lord of their World—Pharaoh, Nebuchadnezzar, and Darius—and how they acted in line with their own law and against the law professed by Faithful. In his judgment, Faithful ought to die. The jury, whose names depicted various vices such as Mr. Blind-man, the foreman, followed by Mr. Malice, Mr. Love-lust, Mr. Cruelty, Mr. Enmity, and a number of others, came to the same conclusion. Consequently, Faithful was condemned to die a cruel death that included whipping, beating, stabbing with both knives and swords, stoning, and finally, burning. The narrator then tells us how he saw two horses and a chariot bring Faithful up into the clouds, taking the fastest way to the gate of Heaven.

Christian escapes from jail and continues with his new companion, Hopeful—Christian was then put back in prison but escaped by the grace of God and went joyfully on his way. He was accompanied by Hopeful, who had been converted by the two pilgrims' steadfast example and claimed that there were more like him who would follow.

By-ends from the town of Fair-speech—Not long after they had left the Fair, they came across another traveler, a man named By-ends (though he didn't tell them that at first) from the town of Fair-speech. Christian had heard that Fair-speech was a wealthy town, which By-ends confirmed along with the fact that he was related to practically the entire town. His ancestors even included the founder of the town, Lord Fair-speech himself, as well as Lord Turn-about, Lord Time-server, Mr. Facing-both-ways, Mr. Smooth-man, and other names indicating hypocrisy and opportunism. Questioning By-ends further, Christian discovered that his wife was the daughter of Lady Feigning and that they prided themselves on their excellent breeding. They were also pleased to appear religious as long as it was convenient and advantageous. By-ends described it as going in Silver Slippers while the sun still shone, and the people approved.

By-ends parts ways with Christian and Hopeful—
At that point, Christian thinks he recognizes him, having heard of him before, and encouraged by Hopeful, he asks By-ends outright to confirm his name. By-ends, however, denies that it is his true name, claiming that others imputed that quality to him but that he was just capitalizing on his good fortune and timing. Christian bluntly replies that the name suits him better than he thinks. He then explains that if he wants to walk with them, he needs to understand that their practice of religion will not always be convenient or profitable and that there will be times when they will have to go against the tide. By-ends, however, is unwilling to discard his principles. They have served him well, and he sees no harm in them; and so, they agree to part ways.

By-ends is joined by others of like mind—By-ends, now walking by himself at some distance behind Christian and Hopeful, is soon approached by a group of like-minded individuals: Misters Hold-the-World, Money-love, and Save-all, who in their youth all attended school with By-ends in the town of Love-gain. They had all studied the Art of Getting under Mr. Gripe-man and each excelled at the various means of acquiring wealth, such as flattery, violence, and lying.

The opportunists justify worldly gain as a worthy religious goal—Money-love then asks By-ends about the two pilgrims ahead, wondering why they chose to walk ahead instead of keeping them company. By-ends explains that their religion is too strict to tolerate differences with others. Curious, Save-all asks about the specific differences. In reply, By-ends describes their insistence on moving ahead on the Way regardless of circumstances or convenience, and of sacrificing, if necessary, all other concerns in the service of God. Mr. Hold-the-World concurs with Mr. By-ends that worldly wealth and wisdom are worthy goals to maintain, supporting his claim with the examples of Abraham, Solomon, and Job.

The examples of the minister and the tradesman—Next, By-ends poses the question of whether it is justifiable and honest to use religion to further an individual's worldly ends, if he sees that he can attain them by no other means. In framing the question, By-ends uses the examples of a minister and a tradesman (as though there were little difference between the two). This prompts Mr. Money-love to address the question in two sections:

The minister example—Suppose, he argues, a minister wants to earn a better living than the meager one he currently has. He may have the idea of preaching more often and more fervently, and it may also seem expedient to him to tailor his sermons more to the needs and preferences of the people. Money-love sees several justifications for this approach, namely, that: 1) there is nothing wrong or illegal about the desire, 2) his preaching improves, as a result, 3) his willingness to adjust his sermons indicates the Christian traits of self-denial and kindness, and 4) by improving upon his resources, he is merely expanding his calling and fulfilling God's Will and should therefore not be judged as greedy.

The tradesman example—The second section of Mr. Money-love's argument deals with more or less the same thing as it applies to a tradesman. Like the minister, the tradesman has the opportunity to improve his income through his association with religion, except that in his case, the improvement comes through an upgrade in the type of people he deals with. If he's lucky, he may even meet and marry a wealthy woman. Money-love sees nothing wrong with any of this. None of it is illegal, and furthermore, he reasons, if religion encourages virtue, what harm can there be in worldly gain—as in a wife, wealth, and good customers—if it comes through the avenue of virtuousness?

The opportunists present their argument to the pilgrims—This reasoning mightily pleased all of his companions so that they decided to pose the question to Christian and Hopeful. And so, they called after them, and Christian and Hopeful graciously waited for them to catch up. Then Mr. Hold-the-World, who had been elected to ask the question, presented it to them with a request for a response.

Christian's answer: those who follow religion for gain will throw it away for the same—Contrary to what they expected, the question did not faze Christian in the least. He answered that to follow Christ for material things (the loaves and the fishes) was a misuse of religion practiced only by heathen, hypocrites, devils, and witches. Of the heathen, he gives the example of Hamor and Sechem, whose only interest in being circumcised was to gain access to Jacob's goods and daughters. The hypocrites were represented by the Pharisees, who made a pretense of piety but secretly went against true religion by plotting ways to acquire the property of widows. The devils' representative was the apostle Judas, whom Christ called a devil and who betrayed Jesus for thirty pieces of silver. And, finally, the witches are represented by Simon Magus, or Simon the Sorcerer, who sought to purchase the power of the Holy Spirit with money and received a sharp rebuke from Peter. Christian concluded his statement with the assertion that those who opted for religion in the name of material gain would discard it for the same reason.

The men in By-end's company were dumbfounded by his reply, which led Christian to wonder how they would deal with God's judgment if they could barely handle the judgment of their fellow man. With that, the two genuine pilgrims went ahead, this time with no argument from the other group.

The Hill Lucre and the Silver Mine—Next, Christian and Hopeful went through a small but pleasant plain called Ease that took them past a hill named Lucre, which contained a silver mine. There, near the mine, sat Demas, who called to them in an effort to entice them from the Way. But Christian, knowing that it was a place where many had been ensnared, and some even died, resisted the invitation in spite of Hopeful's initial interest and Demas' ongoing insistence. Christian had recognized Demas as a deserter whose materialism led to ultimate condemnation, and he, therefore, continued to steadfastly resist. As he and Hopeful continued on their way, they guessed that By-ends and his group would yield to the distraction of the silver mine—and they were right. Exactly what happened to them is unknown, except that they never returned to the path.

The Pillar of Salt—After crossing the plain, they came upon a statue that looked like it had once been a woman. On it was the inscription: Remember Lot's Wife. After Lot and his immediate family (at least, those who had been willing to listen) were rescued from Sodom prior to its destruction, they were warned to not look back as they journeyed onward. But Lot's wife failed to heed the warning, and looking back toward the city as it was being destroyed, she was turned into a pillar of salt. Hopeful and Christian took this as both a warning and an example: a warning to maintain their focus and an example of the destructive consequences if they failed to do so. Hopeful had already experienced how easy it was to be tempted away from the path, since he almost fell into Demas' trap. And Christian pointed out that Lot's wife had already been saved from one disaster but was unable to pass the next test.

The importance of intention—Lot's wife was also an example of the importance of a true pilgrim's mental state. Hopeful wondered why, for example, the group back by the mine could digress without immediate danger while Lot's wife was instantly changed just from looking back. Christian guessed that it had to do with the gravity of the deeds committed in Sodom, which were among the worst. To look back longingly at total depravity indicated a state of mind that would incur a harsh punishment.

The River of the Water of Life—Next, the path went along the River of the Water of Life, as it is called in Revelation 22. The river was flanked by a perpetually green meadow, full of lilies and green fruit trees with healing leaves. Because it was safe there, the pilgrims rested for several days, sleeping, refreshing themselves with the water, nourishing themselves with the fruit, and healing and balancing themselves with the leaves.

By-Path Meadow and the Stile—After that, the path veered away from the river, where it became difficult and rough, so that the pilgrims, whose feet were now sore, found themselves longing for easier treading. They soon came to a meadow, called By-Path Meadow, which was on the other side of a fence separating it from the Way. There was, however, a stile leading over the fence onto another parallel path, and so, since they were weary and the way seemed easier on the other side, Christian suggested that they go over onto the alternate path. Concerned that it would take them out of the Way, Hopeful resisted at first, but Christian convinced him that the two paths were unlikely to veer apart.

The false path leads to a dangerous pit—At first, the alternate path seemed much easier for walking, and seeing another traveler ahead of them, they asked him whether he knew where it went. The traveler, who was called Vain Confidence, told them it led to the Celestial City, and so, reassured by his words, they continued along. However, when night fell, the darkness was so thick that they were unable to see the deep pit that lay ahead. But they did hear Vain Confidence fall, and they heard his groans, at which point Christian wondered if he had made the right choice.

The pilgrims head back in darkness, thunder, and flooding—As they considered what to do next, they were caught in the midst of thunder, lightning, and flooding rain. After Christian apologized to Hopeful and asked for forgiveness, which Hopeful granted, the two began to head back in the darkness. They were further encouraged by a Voice that confirmed their original path as the right Way. As they headed back, the floodwaters rose around them to such an extent that they nearly drowned multiple times.

The pilgrims are seized by the Giant Despair—
Since they were having trouble finding the stile, the pilgrims decided to take refuge under a small shelter. Their weariness got the better of them, though, and before they knew it, they were asleep. To their dismay, they found themselves wakened in the morning by the Giant Despair, whose grounds they had accidentally trespassed on during the night. After questioning them, he took them to Doubting Castle, where he locked them in a dark and foul dungeon without food or water for four days.

The Giant tortures the pilgrims—As he settled into bed the first night of their stay, Giant Despair told his wife Diffidence of the day's events and then asked her what he should do next. After questioning him about the pilgrims' origins and intentions, his wife advised him to beat them mercilessly, which he did. Discovering that they were still alive, his unsatisfied wife suggested that he convince the prisoners to kill themselves. On the following morning, the Giant again dutifully followed the advice of his wife, then lunged at the two pilgrims but in the process suffered from a seizure and was forced to leave.

Hopeful talks Christian out of suicide—Christian and Hopeful, still suffering terribly from their wounds and the abuse of the previous days, began to consider the Giant's idea of suicide. Of the two, Christian was the more convinced, and it was Hopeful who talked him out of it. He first reminded Christian of his duty according to the law (Thou shalt not kill); then, of the complete extinction that awaited those who broke it; of God's power and mercy and the Giant's relative insignificance; and of the probability of escape, judging from the experience of previous prisoners and the likelihood that the Giant would make a mistake.

Again, the Giant returned to check their condition, this time threatening them that things would be even worse. Again, Hopeful tried to dissuade Christian from suicide by reminding him of his prior strength and courage in dealing with Apollyon, of the faith that he showed at Vanity Fair, and of his endurance through all the other trials he had suffered so far. Furthermore, Hopeful counted himself the weaker of the two, yet here in the dungeon, he was able to find the courage, patience, and strength needed to survive. His point was that if he could do it, Christian certainly could, too.

The Giant shows the pilgrims the bones of prior victims—That night, the Giant and his wife again discussed the two prisoners, and this time, his wife suggested showing them the remains of former trespassers, whose bones lay strewn around the castle's exterior. This he did the next day, but with no effect.

After praying, Christian remembers the Key of Promise, which enables them to escape—As the Giant and his wife slept, the two pilgrims prayed, starting at around midnight. Just before dawn, it occurred to Christian that the Key of Promise that he held could open any of the castle's doors. One after the other, the doors of Doubting Castle opened, until the pilgrims reached the Iron Gate, which made such a loud creaking noise that it awoke the Giant, who chased after them. Fortunately, he suffered a seizure, which allowed the pilgrims to escape to the main highway. Once over the stile, they made a sign to warn future pilgrims of the perils of the way on the other side of the fence.

The Delectable Mountains, also known as Emmanuel's Land—The pilgrims' next stop was the Delectable Mountains, the same beautiful mountains they had seen from the Hill Difficulty. They, too, were owned by the Lord of the Hill, and they featured vineyards, gardens, orchards, and fountains, where the pilgrims bathed, nourished, and refreshed themselves. Next to the highway on the mountaintops, the pilgrims could see some Shepherds with their sheep. Upon reaching them, they questioned them about the mountains, the sheep, the Celestial City, and the Way there. The Shepherds explained that both the mountains and the sheep belonged to Emmanuel, the mountains being known as Emmanuel's Land. The pilgrims also learned that, though the Celestial City was near and the Way sure, it was only safe and certain for those who were true but not for those who transgressed.

The Shepherds welcome and instruct the pilgrims—The Shepherds, who were called Knowledge, Experience, Sincere, and Watchful, likewise questioned Christian and Hopeful about their journey. Satisfied with the genuineness of their answers, they welcomed them, feeding and lodging them for the night as their Master expected them to do. The next day, they showed them around the mountains, which contained much that was lovely and inviting but also certain places that functioned as warnings. These were:

- the Hill of Error, where those who deny the bodily resurrection of the dead fall to their deaths
- the Mountain of Caution, where those who climbed over the stile and stumbled onto the Giant's property now stumble blindly amidst the tombs on the mountainside because the Giant put out their eyes

On this second point, the pilgrims said nothing, though they looked at each other and even wept.

The By-way to Hell—The Shepherds then showed them down to a Valley, where from a door in the side of the mountain, the pilgrims could perceive darkness, smoke, the smell of brimstone, and the tormented cries of the Hypocrites who had been consigned to Hell. Some of these had even been on the path a long time, but for one reason or another, they had either sold their souls, betrayed, lied, or blasphemed.

The view of the Celestial Gate and the Shepherds parting blessings—Finally, they led them to a high place called Clear, where they gave them a telescope with which to see the Celestial Gate itself. But Christian and Hopeful were still shaking from their look into Hell, although they managed to catch a glimpse of the Gate. As the pilgrims prepared to move on, the Shepherds sent them away with four blessings: a Note of the Way, a warning about the Flatterer, another warning not to fall asleep on Enchanted Ground, and wishes for a successful journey.

The meeting with Ignorance—Back on the Highway, the two pilgrims passed by the country of Conceit, which lay on the left-hand side of the Way and was connected to it by a crooked path. Coming from there, they encountered a lively young man, also on his way to the Celestial City. This young man, whose name was Ignorance, was convinced that he had all the qualifications to enter through Gate, having led a moral and devout life in his own estimation. But Christian had his doubts since the young man had come onto the Highway by a crooked path instead of through the Wicket Gate. The young man argued that the Wicket Gate lay too far out of the way from his own country and seemed no better than his own pleasant path. Seeing his high opinion of his own wisdom, which rendered him unreceptive, the two pilgrims decided to move ahead and maybe resume their conversation with him at a later date.

The story of Little-Faith, who was assaulted and robbed in Deadman's Lane—Next, they came into a dark road, where they witnessed seven devils taking a man back to the passage to Hell they had seen earlier in the side of the mountain. His sin, which was written on a piece of paper attached to his back, was apostasy, the forsaking of his faith. The sight reminded Christian of another incident that occurred to a man named Little-Faith, who had set out on a pilgrimage from his hometown of Sincere. He had fallen asleep in Deadman's Lane, which proceeded from the Broad-way Gate and was known for the frequency of the murders committed there. In this vulnerable state, he was accosted by three brothers, Mistrust, Guilt, and Faint-heart, who robbed him of practically all his money, though they missed his jewels and his Certificate of entry into the Celestial City. Hearing that others were on their way and being afraid of confronting Great Grace from Good Confidence, the thieves fled, but not before knocking out Little-Faith after he tried to shout for help.

Little-Faith's perseverance and insight—Despite his mishap, Little-Faith persevered for most of the Way, though he often went hungry and had to beg. Hopeful wondered that he hadn't sold his jewels to ease his situation, and for this he received a sharp rebuke from Christian. Unlike Esau, who was easily persuaded by his brother Jacob to sell his birthright for a meal, Little-Faith was aware of the worth of his jewels and would by no means trade them in, knowing that he would not be able to enter the Celestial City without his jewels and his certificate. And this was true despite the fact that the incident with the thieves was so traumatic, being nearly fatal that it had a profoundly negative effect on his attitudes and interactions from then on. His saving grace, however, was his faith, even if it was just a little.

Hopeful's questioning of Little-Faith's courage and the description of Great Grace—Hopeful further wondered why Little-Faith hadn't demonstrated more courage when dealing with the thieves since they were probably no more than a group of cowards. Having been in a similar situation, Christian responded that it was easy to be critical of something you hadn't experienced yourself. Also, since they were Apollyon's lackeys, it seemed to Christian that their King would always be ready to respond to their cries for help, and dealing with Apollyon was extremely difficult. Hopeful reiterated his point, however that as soon as the thieves so much as suspected Great Grace's arrival, they fled, which proved that they were cowards. Christian responded that Little-Faith was no match for Great Grace, who was one of the King's most powerful and outstanding servants and that comparing the two was like comparing a child to a man. And even if Great Grace had arrived, Christian maintained that it still would have been a difficult fight as the scars on Great Grace's face proved.

The danger of trusting in your own strength and the value of Faith—Christian therefore concluded that pilgrims such as he and Hopeful should be cautious in making boastful claims of superior skill and valor. He cited Peter as an example of someone who bragged about his courage and faithfulness yet was easily turned when the time came. He therefore recommends two things when setting out on a dangerous journey: 1) to carry the Shield of Faith, and 2) to request that God himself accompany them. With these two things, he says, no harm can come to them. He personally had already experienced significant danger but could not claim his own strength and skill as the reason for his survival. He ends his argument with a song extolling the protective force of great faith, which in sufficient amount can guard the pilgrim against an army of attackers.

The Flatterer and his snare—As the pilgrims proceeded along the Way, they came to a place where another path connected to the main highway and went parallel to it for as far as they could see. As they were deciding which road to take, they were approached by a black man wearing a light-colored robe, who told them to follow him, since he, too, was going to the Celestial City. The more they followed him, though, the more the path appeared to lead in the wrong direction until they found themselves ensnared in a net, at which point the man's robe fell off to reveal his true color. It was then that the Shepherds' parting instructions came back to them: they were supposed to avoid the Flatterer and read the Note with Directions, both of which they forgot to do.

The pilgrims are rescued and chastised by a Shining One—Not knowing what to do, they lay entangled for a while until the arrival of a Shining One, a radiant being, who first asked them the usual questions. Then, after releasing them, he explained that it had been the Flatterer who misled them. After leading them back to the true path, he asked them some more questions, and finally, having deduced that they did not listen to the Shepherds' instructions, he whipped them soundly so that they would not forget their mistake and then sent them on their way.

The meeting with Atheist—Grateful for the lesson, they continued on the path until they met someone named Atheist. On asking them where they were going, he laughed them to scorn when they told him, informing them that there was no such place. He claimed to have gone farther than they and found nothing, so now he was heading back. But Christian and Hopeful recognized the man for another Flatterer, and having seen the Celestial Gate from the Delectable Mountains, they chose to continue in faith.

The Enchanted Ground and Hopeful's story of his conversion—As they came to the land of the Enchanted Ground, Hopeful began to feel drowsy, and not remembering the third Shepherd's warning, he suggested they take a nap. Fortunately, Christian did recall the admonishment and promptly reminded Hopeful of the danger of sleeping in that area. He suggested that, to avoid drowsiness, they should engage in an engaging and fruitful discussion. Christian, therefore, began by asking Hopeful how he had come to take up the path of Salvation. Hopeful answered that he had once been smitten with the things of this world, in addition to being prone to riotous living. In fact, his conversion first came about through Christian and Faithful's preaching and example. When asked if he had had an immediate conversion, Hopeful answered "no." The effect had been gradual, with significant resistance on his part owing to

- his ignorance of how God worked

- the pleasure he still derived from sinning and from likeminded company

- the torment he experienced thinking about it

When asked what made him think about his sins, Hopeful gave eight specific answers that more or less fell into four broad categories:

- a reminder of good, such as meeting a good person or hearing the words of the Bible

- personal pain (in the form of a headache)

- the sickness or death of others

- thoughts of his own death, and worst of all, of his judgment

Hopeful's attempts to save himself—Christian then asked Hopeful how he eased his conscience, to which Hopeful replied that he put his old friendships behind him and took up a life of devotion and good deeds. When asked whether that had the desired effect, Hopeful replied that it did at first, but this was temporary. Through Biblical teachings, he began to gain an awareness of a righteousness higher than his own and that his own righteousness was in any case inadequate to repay his former debt of sinfulness, even with total reform. Moreover, even his best actions seemed tainted with a new kind of sinfulness, which left him wondering what, if anything, he could do to redeem himself.

The conversation with Faithful—Finally, he spoke to Faithful, a close acquaintance of his, who told him that he would have to attain the righteousness of one who was absolutely free of sin, past and present. He further explained that the only one with those qualifications was Jesus Christ, whose divine status enabled him to redeem others through his sacrifice on the Cross. If Hopeful believed in Jesus Christ, then he, too, would partake of Christ's perfect righteousness.

Resistance to the idea of Grace—At first, Hopeful resisted the idea, thinking himself unworthy. Faithful then counseled him to ask Jesus, which Hopeful again resisted, since it seemed presumptuous to him. But Faithful insisted that Jesus himself extended the invitation, and he gave him a book that proved it. At Hopeful's request, he also showed him how to pray to him and what to say, for Christ was always ready to pardon sincere and fervent seekers.

The message to be patient and wait—So Hopeful did as he was told many, many times, but without any immediate effect. Often, he considered giving up, but his belief was so strong that he continued in prayer. At one point, he received a mental message to the effect that if nothing was happening, to simply wait, and eventually, his request would be answered.

The vision of Christ—One day, when Hopeful was deeply depressed because of the magnitude of his sins and his conviction that he would be damned to Hell, he thought he saw Jesus telling him that he would be saved if he believed. Hopeful protested that he was too great a sinner, but Christ reassured him with his grace. Hopeful then asked what it meant to believe, to which Christ answered that believing and coming were one and the same, and that those who came to him would never hunger or thirst.

The recognition and experience of Grace—After further questioning and with tears in his eyes, Hopeful learned that Jesus, as the Son of God, had come to save the world from condemnation and that this was why he died and resurrected and continues to mediate on our behalf. That realization, which Christian deemed a true revelation from Christ, filled Hopeful's heart with love, joy, and gratitude for Christ and all things proceeding from him; and at the same time, it gave him a horror of the memory of his former life and a deep desire to live his life in the name of Christ.

The second conversation with Ignorance—When Hopeful was finished relating his experience to Christian, he happened to look back and see that Ignorance was still following them, though at a distance. Hopeful suggested that they wait for him, which they did despite Christian's argument that Ignorance would have no interest in their company. Still, they waited, and when he caught up, Christian inquired about his well-being. Ignorance replied that he was well, since his thoughts were perpetually focused on God and heaven, to which Christian replied that the same was true of devils and the damned. Ignorance countered that the difference was that he truly desired them, but again Christian argued that a slothful person might desire things yet possess nothing. Ignorance then claimed that he had forsaken all for them. This Christian doubted because of the great difficulty involved. Nevertheless, he asked Ignorance what led him to believe that, to which Ignorance answered that the message came from his heart. To this, Christian answered that a man should never trust in his own heart but should place his faith in the Word of God. A person's heart could easily deceive, which was why to trust it would be foolish. Furthermore, contrary to Ignorance's assertion that a man's heart could be good, the Word of God stated the opposite—that the natural man was evil from the day he was born and that only when he began to recognize that would his thoughts be in line with those of God. The same was true for the natural man's estimation of his ways, which were inherently evil in the sight of God. Furthermore, our thoughts of God should be in line with His own Word, which states that His knowledge of us is deeper and more thorough than our own and that our righteousness is nothing in His sight.

Justification by Faith through the righteousness of Christ—Here Ignorance took offense at Christian's view of him as lacking humility before God, since he, too, believes that he must be justified by Christ. Christian, however, is not convinced, as that would require feeling his need for Christ because of his sinfulness. Ignorance believes that his dutiful performance of the law will be justified by Christ and made acceptable to the Father. To Christian, however, Ignorance suffers from an erroneous understanding. He argues that his faith is a fantasy with no basis in the divine Word; a falsity, since it is based on the righteousness of the individual rather than that of Christ; and mistaken in its understanding of justification, which it sees as the justification of the person on the basis of his own righteous actions instead of through the being of Christ. He adds that true justification involves not the redemption of the individual because of his own obedience but because of Christ's obedience to God's law and his consequent suffering. This seems nonsensical to Ignorance, who concludes that the believer, without the guidance of the law, could easily go astray. Christian counters that his argument shows how little he knows of the Grace of God, which, when experienced, changes the heart, thus providing true redemption.

Ignorance parts ways with the Christian and Hopeful over the notion of Grace—At this point, Hopeful suggests asking Ignorance whether he has ever experienced this Saving Grace. Ignorance quickly interjects that his opinion of their sense of revelation is that it is pure foolishness, to which Hopeful replies that it must seem so to him, since it is hidden from the natural man. Christian agrees with Hopeful and urges Ignorance to admit his sinfulness and allow the Grace of God, which is the only means of revelation and redemption, to work its saving effects on him. But to Ignorance, this is all too fast, and he, therefore, elects again to remain behind, since he cannot keep up with the other two pilgrims.

So Christian and Hopeful went their way alone again, feeling sorry for Ignorance and others like him, of which there were many even among those who held themselves for true believers. According to Christian, their primary flaw lay in their suppression of the sense of sin within themselves, which in his opinion stood to benefit them if they could face it rather than deluding themselves about their condition.

The concept of "right fear"—Christian and Hopeful then discussed the advantages of "right" fear, which they defined as 1) arising from the conviction of sin within oneself, 2) seeking Christ as the saving solution, and 3) the awakening of a deep love and reverence for God and his way, making the soul particularly sensitive and fearful of any transgressions. In his view, the ignorant make four basic mistakes with regard to a right sense of fear. First, they believe that it comes from Satan rather than God, its true Source. Second, they believe that their faith will be ruined if they give in to it. For these reasons, they try to fend off their fears, and that in turn leads them to the final two mistakes: the cultivation of a false sense of confidence and a conviction of their own holiness.

The backsliding of Temporary—After Hopeful confirms that he has experienced these things, Christian suggests moving on to a different topic—the plight of a man named Temporary, whom Hopeful had also known for a while. Temporary had experienced an awakening to his own sinfulness and need for redemption but then changed his mind about making a pilgrimage when he came in contact with a person named Saveself.

Why people backslide

Hopeful believed there were four reasons for this sort of backsliding:

- insufficient conviction to carry him through to the final goal of reaching the Celestial Gate
- the fear of men and of worldly troubles
- a low opinion of true religion
- a dislike of facing the guilt and terror that accompany the spiritual path

How people backslide

Christian then details how they go about their backsliding, namely:

- They avoid thinking about death, judgment, or God.
- They cease practicing the elements of a spiritual life, such as watchfulness, praying in secret, self-abnegation, and so on.
- They avoid the company of genuine Christians, who are characterized by their warmth and enthusiasm.
- They drop their public spiritual obligations, such as attending church and other religious meetings.

- They backbite serious practitioners of religion.
- They cultivate the company of reckless and immoral people.
- They look for immoral actions in the example of supposedly moral people so that they can justify the same lifestyle for themselves, which they secretly begin to lead.
- They begin to openly lead a corrupt lifestyle by small degrees.
- They openly go the full route, having now been utterly hardened, thereby guaranteeing their own destruction.

In short, having been primarily motivated by their fear of Hell, their desire for Heaven is too weak to motivate them to continue on the path. To this, Christian adds that they do not have a true distaste for sin but only a fear of punishment.

The land called Beulah—To their delight, the pilgrims finally emerged from the Enchanted Ground into a land called Beulah,[1] a place of sunshine, flowers, birdsong, and an abundance of everything good and needful—a land beyond death, doubt, and despair, with a clear view of the Celestial City. Because it is so near the City, it is not unusual to see the Shining Ones here or to hear encouraging voices coming from the City. From here, the pilgrims could see that the City was made of pearls and gemstones, with streets of gold, which created such a state of desire in both Christian and Hopeful that they both felt ill and had to rest a bit. Later, continuing on the Way, they came to gardens, vineyards, and orchards just alongside the main path. As they approached, they were met by the gardener. He explained that the gardens and orchards belonged to the King, who welcomed pilgrims and invited them to nourish, replenish, and rest themselves there.

---

[1] A term meaning "bride," or "married." It is found in Isaiah 62 in reference to the transition from a state of forsakenness to one of protection and union with God. The concepts of marriage and of the desolate land turned into fruitful country also signifies that state of spiritual attainment that approaches the pinnacle of the development of the soul, in which the person experiences permanent health, holiness, and happiness.

Christian and Hopeful set out toward the Celestial City—After they slept, they set their faces toward the City but found it difficult to look at it directly because of its extreme radiance, and they had to use a special instrument. As they approached, they encountered two radiant beings, men dressed in gold with shining faces. These men asked them the usual questions about the details of their journey and then informed them that they had to undergo two more trials before they could enter the City. They agreed to accompany the two pilgrims but stressed that their passage into the City had to be obtained on the strength of their own faith.

The River with no bridge—Next Christian, Hopeful, and their two companions came to a deep river immediately before the base of the hill leading to the Celestial Gate. The two guides informed the pilgrims that they had to cross the river to enter the City. Dismayed because there was no bridge, the pilgrims began to look for another way. They were informed that, though there was another path, it had been barred to all except Elijah and Enoch, and it would continue to be so until Resurrection Day.

Hopeful bolsters Christian's faith in God and Christ—Christian, who was the more dismayed and doubting of the two, asked if the river's waters were all of one depth, to which the guides replied that the depth varied according to the person's faith in the King. Almost immediately upon entering the river, Christian began to sink and drown. Hopeful, however, found solid ground to stand on and constantly tried to reassure Christian. But Christian, who was deeply troubled and bewildered by the memory of all his sins and the appearance of evil spirits, could not muster the faith that God was there with him, and so he continued to drown until Hopeful counseled and encouraged him enough that he understood that it was a test and was able to muster sufficient faith in God and Christ to get across.

The ascent to the City—Once on the other side, they were again met by the same two shining beings who had led them there, who now announced themselves as helpers and guides to those who would inherit salvation. The pilgrims' next task was to ascend the hill to the City, which was situated above the clouds. Still, the pilgrims climbed it with ease, having shed their earthly, destructible garments and being supported by their radiant guides.

The Shining Ones describe the celestial state—As they walked, the guides explained to them the glorious nature of the place and that they were about to enter a land of perfection and immortality. All suffering and death would be removed, they would commune with the King daily from now on, and they would be clothed in white robes and golden crowns, joining the prophets, patriarchs, and their friends who had gone before them. Now they would reap the benefits of the toil and sufferings they had previously undergone, and now, too, they would rejoice over those who followed and, together with the King, judge those who had tormented them.

Christian and Hopeful are welcomed to the Celestial City—As they approached the heavenly Gate, they were joyfully surrounded by a welcoming host of angels, who greeted them with shouts and trumpet sounds that mixed with the tolling of bells from the Celestial City itself. Once at the Gate, they were instructed to call and then hand in their Certificates to Enoch, Moses, and Elijah, who brought them to the King, who in turn read them and admitted the pilgrims. As they passed through the Gate, they were changed and received radiant, golden clothing, along with harps and crowns, and again, the sound of ringing bells could be heard throughout the City.

Ignorance is transported to Hell—As the narrator was admiring the glorious City and its radiant inhabitants, he saw Ignorance approach and then cross the river with relative ease, having received the help of the ferryman, Vain-Hope. Once over, he ascended the hill to the Gate, though without the guidance or welcome given to the two pilgrims. At the Gate, he was questioned and asked for his Certificate, which he was unable to produce. And so, Ignorance was bound and flown straight to the door in the hill that led to Hell—directly from the Gate of Heaven. And with that, the dream ends.

CONCLUSION

The narrator's final words of advice to readers—
The narrator ends with a brief warning to not misinterpret the dream, since that can only lead to evil. He adds to not get too entangled in the externals or to succumb to either ridicule or rage, and to leave that to either fools or those who are too young to understand. Instead, focus on the inner meaning, the heart of the allegory. If you approach the story honestly, you will be rewarded with worthwhile meaning. The narrator humbly counsels that if you find anything unworthy, simply toss it; but be careful not to throw out the gold with the dross—or else, you may force him to dream again.

Part II: Introduction

In the opening section of Part 2, the narrator introduces us to Christiana and her children, who are now following in Christian's footsteps, having left the world and embarked on the Way of the pilgrim. They have already experienced many of the hardships of pilgrimage but also the joys, and it is clear that they have committed themselves to the final goal as established by their Lord.

The four sections of the introduction—The rest of the introduction is divided into four sections containing an objection and an answer. The author is addressing the book he is about to write, which is the sequel to the first allegory, so the interchange in these four sections is between the new book and the author.

Section 1: Proof of authenticity—In the first section, the concern is about how readers will know the sequel to be an authentic version, since numerous copycat works have been produced. The author answers by saying it will be known by its language, the plain talk of Puritanism that was not widely used and was difficult to imitate.

Section 2: The book's universal popularity—In the second section, the book asks what it should do if it comes to a place where its message is hated. The author answers to not worry about such things—that the original book is highly prized and beloved worldwide, across culture, gender, and age. Even those who rejected it at first have been known to love and value it upon further engagement.

Section 3: Objections to the content—The third section deals with various objections to the material itself. To the criticism that the pilgrim laughs too much, the author answers that his laughter has to be understood in the context of his tears—of an emotional and spiritual experience that runs deeper than may appear on the surface. To the criticism that the pilgrim's head is in a cloud (also worded in the original as "A Cloud is in his Head"), the author answers that profound wisdom often seems obscure at first but that those who seek Divine Wisdom are more apt to research and ponder such things. The so-called "darkness" of the book's stories seems to refer to the use of allegory rather than straightforward speech, judging from the author's answer to this criticism, which says that people are more likely to remember stories than logical arguments. The author, therefore, sums up this section by telling the book not to worry and furthermore that Christiana will furnish whatever Christian missed.

Section 4: Objections to the form—In the fourth section, the objection continues with regard to the subject of allegory, which some find objectionable. Here, the author addresses the book directly as Christiana, the new protagonist, telling her that if she should meet with those who object to the book's form, she should return blessing for cursing, love for hatred, according the spirit of the Way itself. He urges her to be tolerant of people's preferences and to focus on those who are receptive to the book's message and method.

Introduction to the pilgrims of Part II—He further instructs her to introduce those she meets to her companions in the Way, Mercy and Honest. Mercy has been her companion for a long time and stands as a shining example of innocence and purity, especially in young girls. On the other end of the spectrum is the elderly Honest, whose forthright, simple, and dedicated ways may inspire some older folk to shed their sinfulness and lovingly follow Christ.

Finally, the author encourages Christiana to tell people of the trials and special challenges of different pilgrims. There was Master Fearing, whose goodness won him the ultimate prize, though he walked alone and was often sad. Then there was Master Feeble-mind, a man with a true love for the Divine, though his spirit was weak. He would follow behind and once had his life saved by Great-heart. Master Feeble-mind walked with his lame friend, Master Ready-to-halt, and despite their infirmities, they were sometimes known to break out singing and dancing. Next, there was Master Valiant-for-Truth, a young man who, together with Great-heart, slew the Giant Despair and destroyed Doubting Castle. Finally, there were Master Despondency and his daughter Much-afraid, who on the surface seemed forsaken, yet in the end rejoiced in the steadfastness of their Lord.

Bunyan gives the book his blessing as he sends it out into the world—At this point, the author reverts to addressing the book directly instead of through its main character, Christiana. He sends it off into the world with its mission to elevate and heal the good and to destroy the bad. And if its mysteries still remain hidden to the average soul, then may they be left for those with greater spiritual gifts to unravel. He ends this opening section with his blessing upon the book and the hope that it will both be of value to those already on the path and turn others to the right Way.

Part II

The narrator meets Mr. Sagacity at the beginning of his dream—The sequel to *The Pilgrim's Progress* was written a few years after Bunyan wrote the first book. By this time, he had been released from jail and was once more working as a tinker. Again, it is narrated as a dream: the narrator falls asleep and awakens in a dream state, where he meets an elderly gentleman, Mr. Sagacity, in the forest. As they set out on their journey together, the narrator questions his companion about a large city down below on the left side of the hill. Mr. Sagacity answers that it is the City of Destruction, confirming the narrator's suspicions. Both are also aware that the population there is somewhat lazy and undisciplined. Noticing that his friend does not enjoy describing people in a negative manner, the narrator guesses that he is a man of goodwill and asks him whether he has heard of Christian and his journey. Mr. Sagacity confirms that he certainly has, along with all the sufferings he endured along the Way. But now, they both agree, he is beyond all that, in a place that knows neither sorrow, suffering, nor toil. Furthermore, he has gained the good graces of both the King and the Prince of that City, he has constant access to the Fountain of Life, and his new companions are the same Shining Ones who appear as guides on the journey of every good pilgrim. Once derided by the people of the City of Destruction, Christian is now spoken of with great admiration.

Christiana's change of heart—The narrator then inquires about Christian's wife and children and discovers that though they first resisted the idea of Christian's journey, they have now changed their minds and have left on their own pilgrimage. So Mr. Sagacity begins to tell the narrator of the change that took place in Christiana's heart after permanently losing her husband once he had crossed the great River. She and her husband had loved each other, but she had hardened herself to his pleas and now felt remorse for the way she treated him and for his general sufferings at the time. She had misjudged the reasons for his desire to set out on his journey, and so, thinking him foolish and depressed, and fearing the troubles he would encounter, she had prevented herself and her children from going with him to attain the Source of all true and permanent Life. Now she saw that he had been right, and though the Way still lay open to her and her sons, she would have to navigate it without his help or company.

Christiana's strange dreams and visions—Then Christiana experienced a series of strange dreams and occurrences. First, she dreamt that she saw a parchment containing a description of all her sins, which made her cry out for mercy in the middle of the night. Next, there appeared two horrid-looking beings by her bed, who were discussing her fate between themselves. They felt that she belonged to them, so their goal was to prevent her from becoming a pilgrim so that Hell would not lose her soul. This left her sweating and shaking, but on falling asleep again, she dreamt of Christian in Heaven, surrounded by immortals and bowing before a throne, on which was seated a Prince whose head was crowned by a rainbow.

A messenger from the Immortal Realm delivers a letter of invitation to Christiana—The next day, there was a knock at the door by one who had been sent from the Immortal Realm to inform Christiana that her remorse and prayers had been heard. The merciful God had sent a messenger to invite her, and her children to take the same journey as her husband. The messenger, therefore, handed her a letter, written in gold and with the most heavenly scent. It was an invitation from the King himself to embark on the Way leading to the Celestial City, as her husband had done. Overwhelmed, she asked the messenger whether he would carry them there, but he firmly replied that the bitterness of the Way had to precede the blessings of Heaven. The messenger then advised her to keep the letter safe near her breast, except when reading and memorizing the song it contained along the Way, for she and her children would be singing this to the King. Furthermore, it was her key for entering the Celestial Kingdom. Her first task then would be to enter the Way through the Wicket Gate, which she would reach by crossing the Plain. With this, the messenger wished her a good journey, and after she had called her sons together to explain their next move, he bid them all goodbye.

The visit of Mrs. Timorous and Mercy, Christiana's neighbors—As they were preparing to leave, there was another knock at the door, and as she had done with the first visitor, Christiana bid the person enter if they came in the name of God. In fact, it was two of Christiana's neighbors, and though they were somewhat bewildered by her statement, being unused to such speech from her, they decided to come in anyway. On learning of her intentions, Mrs. Timorous (the daughter of the same Timorous fled the lions on the Hill Difficulty) did her best to dissuade Christiana by pointing out all the hardship she would face along the Way. Although Christiana had shown her the letter, given her reasons, and instructed her that suffering had to precede joy, Mrs. Timorous interpreted it all as insanity.

Mercy's compassion and yearning—The other neighbor, however, was not so convinced. Her name was Mercy, and her heart went out to Christiana as she listened to her story. While Mrs. Timorous scorningly washed her hands of Christiana's "madness," Mercy decided that she would help her at least for part of the Way, and in secret, she longed to know more to see if she herself might not also make the pilgrimage.

Mrs. Timorous gossips with the neighbors—Being a busybody, Mrs. Timorous could not keep the story to herself and instead rounded up her neighbors, Mistresses Bat's-eyes, Light-mind, Inconsiderate, and Know-nothing. It was clear to them that what they counted foolishness—that the bitter had to precede the sweet—was to Christiana an even stronger impetus for action. Mrs. Light-mind also emphasized how many of the townspeople—among them, Mistresses Wanton, Love-the-Flesh, and Filth as well as Mr. Lechery—enjoyed the things of this world and would rather not concern themselves with irrelevant subjects.

Christiana invites Mercy to join them on the Way—In the meantime, Mercy, Christiana, and her children had already set out on their journey. Moved by young Mercy's compassion and glad to have her company, Christiana offered to pay her way as a servant and to inquire at the Wicket Gate of the likelihood of her being welcomed at the Celestial City as a member of her group, even though she had no invitation of her own. To this, Mercy agreed but then began to be tearful at the remembrance of her lost relatives in the City of Destruction. Seeing her merciful nature at work once again, Christiana commended her and encouraged her with the knowledge that she, too, had once been in the position of Mercy's relatives but that God had been merciful to her and her children and had sent for her and opened the way for her salvation. This strengthened Mercy's faith and love so that they continued on together.

Crossing the Slough of Despond—Next, Christiana and her company came to the Slough of Despond. Recognizing it as one of the places where her husband had fallen in and gotten stuck, Christiana hesitated. But Mercy encouraged her to go on, and so they crossed, being cautious to follow the Steps; and though Christiana almost fell in several times, they made it safely to the other side. Here, Mr. Sagacity, who had told the story thus far, parted ways with the narrator, now left to dream by himself.

Arrival at the Wicket Gate, the ferocious dog, and the Keeper's welcome—Once the little group made it to the Wicket Gate, they elected Christiana to knock at the Gate and be their spokesperson. This she did, but instead of finding the Gatekeeper, they were accosted by a large, barking dog. Frightened, they quit knocking for a while until, not knowing what else to do, they tried again. This time, they were greeted by the Keeper, who asked them the usual questions—where they were from and what they wanted. Bowing low, Christiana introduced herself and her children and stated their purpose. Amazed that one who had been so opposed to her husband's pilgrimage had now taken up the path, the Keeper let her and her children in and instructed the trumpeter above the Gate to sound the notes of his trumpet with joy.

Mercy, who was left outside, pleads for entrance—
Mercy, however, still stood outside, upset at the thought of rejection, so Christiana's next move was to intercede for her. Growing increasingly impatient and afraid, Mercy began knocking loudly until the Gatekeeper answered, but by then she had fainted from weakness. Seeing this, the keeper took her hand and bid her arise. She protested that she was too weak, but he encouraged her with the verse: "When my soul fainted, I remembered the Lord …" Instructing her to set aside her fears, he again told her to rise and state her purpose. This she did but confessed that she had no invitation except from Christiana. Then she humbly requested that if there were any mercy to spare that she, too, might be admitted. As he gently led her, the Keeper comforted her with the words that he would intercede for all who believed on him, regardless of why they had come. He then gave her myrrh to relieve her swooning.

The Keeper's forgiveness of their sins and the discussion in the parlor—Once they had all been received by the gentle and compassionate Keeper, the first thing they did was to express their deep remorse for their sins and to ask for pardon. This he immediately gave, assuring them both with his words and by virtue of his sacrifice on the Cross, which he showed them from the top of the Wicket Gate. After that, he left them by themselves in an open-air parlor, where they discussed how happy they were that they had all been admitted through the Gate and had made it past the ferocious barking dog. Mercy had been especially afraid that she would be left behind, especially after hearing the dog. Yet in spite of feeling weak, she took heart when she saw the words above the Gate, which encouraged pilgrims to knock, promising that the Gate would be opened. Mercy's statement that she had been hesitant surprised Christiana because her knocking had been so urgent. In fact, Mercy feared that it had sounded rude, but Christiana said that the Gatekeeper had smiled when he heard it, with no sign of annoyance.

Mercy asks about the ferocious barking dog—When the Keeper returned to the parlor, Mercy asked on behalf of all why he kept such a horrible dog. He explained that the dog was not his and that its owner's purpose was to frighten away the pilgrims, who were the only ones who could hear its barking. But, he added, had she known even a little bit of his power and protection, she would never have been afraid of the dog. After that, Mercy acknowledged his perfection.

The Keeper sends the pilgrims on their way—And so, having cleansed their feet and fed them, the Gatekeeper sent the pilgrims on their journey to follow the steps he had laid out for them in the Way.

The boys eat the fruit from the enemy's garden—Now next to the Way was a wall, and on the other side was a garden belonging to the dog's owner, who was also the Gatekeeper's, and therefore the pilgrims', enemy. Growing across the wall were the branches of some fruit trees, and since the fruit looked appetizing and had fallen to the ground, and since the pilgrims didn't know to whom it belonged, the boys started to pick it up and eat it. This usually brought terrible results, and their mother, Christiana, scolded them, but they ignored her.

The two rapists—As the little group continued along the Way, the women noticed two hideous men coming toward them, so they placed their veils over their heads and kept their focus on the road. As the men neared them, they honed in on the women, as though they wanted to take them by force. Christiana firmly told them to back off and keep going, but they ignored her, so she kicked them, with Mercy also joining in to the best of her ability. Unable to fend off their attackers, they screamed, and when relief came from the Keeper's house, which was still within earshot, the two would-be rapists fled over the wall into the enemy's garden, where they had the protection of the ferocious barking dog.

The Reliever promises to request a Guide for the pilgrims—After establishing that the women and children were all right, the Reliever asked them why they had not requested a guide for their journey and spared themselves these sorts of problems. Christiana answered that, content with their blessings at the time, it had not occurred to them, just as it had not occurred to them that troubles of this sort could come so near the Gatekeeper's house. When she asked whether they should return to request one, the Reliever said that he would present their case to the Keeper and that it was not necessary for them to return personally. Moreover, they would find the resting places built for pilgrims along the Way furnished with everything they would need for their protection on their journey. Nevertheless, there were times, as in this case, when a particular request was needed to guarantee that the gift would be valued. Having explained things to the women, the Reliever departed, leaving them to continue on the path.

Lessons learned from the incident—As they journeyed onward, they discussed the lessons they had learned from the incident. Mercy, in her youth and innocence, confessed to being surprised that they should experience any more sorrow or suffering from this point. Christiana, however, related it to the dream she had had of the two ill-favored men who had appeared by her bedside and discussed how to prevent her from succeeding on her pilgrimage so that they would not lose her, too, as they had lost her husband. She held herself responsible for her lack of foresight, having known on some level that this would occur. Mercy, however, also found in the incident an occasion for gratitude and wonder at the abundance of grace shown them by their Lord.

Arrival at the Interpreter's House—Late in the day, they came upon the Interpreter's house, and drawing near, they could hear voices inside conversing in positive terms about Christiana and the fact that she, who had been previously opposed, had now undertaken a pilgrimage. Finally, she knocked at the door and requested lodging, explaining to the young woman who answered that they understood that the house was a significant resting place for pilgrims. On being asked her name, she introduced herself as Christiana, wife of a previous pilgrim, Christian, and that she, her four sons, and her friend were also all pilgrims.

The Interpreter's household welcomes and instructs Christiana and her party—Joyful and excited at the news, the young woman, whose name was Innocent, ran to call the other members of the household. When the Interpreter himself arrived at the door, he verified Christiana's identity, rejoicing at her conversion from stubborn hardheartedness to willing pilgrimage. Welcoming them all in, the household members bid them rest, and then, while supper was being prepared, the Interpreter showed them around the house, where they witnessed the same scenes as Christian before them.

The man with the muckrake—Once the pilgrims had pondered the things they had seen in the house, the Interpreter brought them to a room with a man who held a muckrake in his hand while looking perpetually downwards. As he raked up straws, sticks, and dust, another man stood above him, holding a Celestial Crown, which he offered him instead. But the muckraker ignored him as he continued to collect the dirt and sticks.

Without prompting, Christiana immediately guessed that the muckraker symbolized a man of this world. The Interpreter confirmed her statement, adding that the muckrake signified the carnal mind and that those who overly concern themselves with material goals lose their desire for Heaven, believing the things of this world to be real and worthwhile and Heaven to be a mere fiction.

The spider in the best room of the house—Next, he took them into the best room in the house, which was, however, entirely empty except for one large spider on the wall. Asking them to look around and tell him what they saw, Mercy at first said she saw nothing, while Christiana declined to say anything. With further prompting from the Interpreter, Mercy noticed the spider. When he asked whether she could see more than one, Christiana intervened, saying that, yes, there was indeed more than one and that they were far more poisonous than the one on the wall. Pleased that she had begun to grasp the symbolism, the Interpreter explained it further as meaning that no matter how much a person might be suffering from the poison of sin, the power of Faith could still guide that individual to the best room of the Celestial House.

The hen and her chicks—After that, he led them into a room with a hen and her brood of chicks. This room contained two lessons. The first was that every time the hen drank water, she would look upward, meaning that every time a pilgrim received a favor, she should remember its Source. The second lesson was that the hen had four different calls: a common call, a special call, a brooding note, and an outcry. The hen was likened to God, the chicks to the faithful, and the four calls to the four divine methods of drawing people to Himself. The common call, which goes on all the time, dispenses nothing; the distinctive call brings with it a gift; the brooding note is reserved for those under his protection; and the outcry alerts His children to danger. The Interpreter further adds that he specifically brought them into that room because, being women, they could easily grasp the concepts.

The patient sheep—Next, he took them into a room where a sheep was being slaughtered. The sheep, however, suffered her fate patiently and quietly, without complaint. This, according to the Interpreter, was how they were meant to take their sufferings.

The garden of many flowers—Next, he took them into the garden, where he showed them many different flowers, some more impressive or beautiful than others, yet each content with its own gifts and location, according to the gardener's design.

The poor crop—From there, he brought them to a field that had been planted with wheat and corn, yet now contained only straw because the tops had been removed. He told them that the ground had been thoroughly prepared but that the crop had still not turned out well. When he asked what they should do with such a crop, Christiana suggested burning and composting it. The Interpreter left them with the lesson that they should beware that they did not end up like the crop in the field.

The robin with the spider—As they returned to the house, they saw a robin holding a spider in its beak. To Christiana, that seemed disappointing since she had always seen robins as attractive, harmless birds that enjoyed human company and fed on such things as breadcrumbs. The Interpreter noted that the robin was teaching them a lesson: that some folk might seem devout and sincere, preferring the company of true believers and acting appropriately in public, but when they were alone, they fell into more depraved patterns.

The Interpreter teaches the pilgrims proverbs— Back at the house, they saw that dinner was still being prepared, so in the meantime, Christiana requested further instruction from the Interpreter. He obliged with a number of useful proverbs as summarized by the following:

- The healthier a strong man, the more he tends toward sinfulness.
- To be adorned with spiritual things is worth more in the sight of God than all ornaments and stylish apparel.
- To start on the Way is easy, but the real test is to finish the course.
- Only those who care for the things of God will let go of the good things of this world.
- As a single leak will sink an entire ship, so can one sin destroy a person.
- To forget your Savior is to condemn yourself.
- Those who seek happiness through sin are like those who expect to grow wheat by planting weeds.
- Live each day as though it were your last.
- Gossip and hypocrisy are signs of depravity.
- If the things that men value are counted as nothing in God's sight, then how precious must be the things that God esteems?
- If this life, with all its sufferings, is so hard to let go of, what must Heaven be like?
- All recognize the good that men do, but who vouches for God's Goodness?
- The needs of this world are temporary, but the needs of the heavenly world are eternally fulfilled in Christ.

The rotten tree—Then the Interpreter led them back into the garden to look at a tree that on the outside seemed healthy, but that was rotten on the inside. This was another metaphor for hypocrites, who seemed holy and devout on the outside, yet on the inside were full of vice and therefore destined for Hell. Finally, dinner was ready, and while they all ate, the Interpreter called for music and singing, as was his usual custom.

The Interpreter asks Christiana about the beginning of her journey—After the song of praise and gratitude for God's support, the Interpreter asked Christiana what had motivated her to go on a pilgrimage. To this, she gave several answers, namely: 1) grief over losing her husband; 2) guilt and remorse over her original hardheartedness toward his sufferings along the Way; 3) the dream of his happiness in Heaven; and 4) the visitation by the messenger with the letter of invitation from the King of the Celestial City. Next, the Interpreter asked whether no one had opposed her leaving. She replied that Mrs. Timorous had tried to dissuade her with tales of danger and difficulty and by calling her plan foolish, but her efforts had no effect. Then she told him of the hideous pair of beings that had stood by her bedside and later accosted them in the Way. This, she said, still troubled her.

The Interpreter asks Mercy the same question—In spite of Christiana's concerns, the Interpreter applauded her for an excellent start, which was, therefore, likely to have a good end. He then turned to Mercy and asked her the same question. Embarrassed and fearful of being found inadequate, Mercy said nothing for while. On further prompting from the Interpreter, she confessed her lack of experience and a dearth of both dreams and visions. Yet when she heard Christiana speak of her reasons for leaving, she felt a burning in her heart and a desire to leave all and go with her. Her only grief was that she had left her relatives behind, but she knew that there was nothing left to expect in her hometown except destruction. Hearing all this, the Interpreter likened her to Ruth, who out of pure love left her home country to follow Naomi wherever she went. That night, Mercy could hardly sleep for joy, since now, more than ever, she felt that she would be accepted.

Final preparations for the journey—At dawn the next morning, as they were preparing to leave, the Interpreter convinced them to first bathe. He then instructed Innocent to take them to the bath in the garden, where she washed them clean from all the dirt they had accumulated during their journey. Aside from cleansing them, the water from the bath also invigorated them and gave their joints additional strength. Following that, the Interpreter set a seal between their eyes so that those they would meet on their journey would recognize them. It was a special seal that contained the Passover eaten by the children of Israel before fleeing Egypt, and it greatly beautified and glorified their faces, giving them an angelic appearance. Next, he had Innocent bring them a change of clothing—clean, white linen garments that made each woman appear more beautiful and glorious to the other than to her own self.

The Interpreter provides a Guide and bids the pilgrims farewell—Finally, the Interpreter called his servant Great-heart, who armed himself with a helmet, shield, and sword in order to accompany the women to their next stop, the great house whose name was Beautiful, situated on the Hill of Difficulty. As the Interpreter's household cheerfully bid them goodbye, the party of pilgrims set off on their journey, singing of their latest adventure and the lessons they learned.

The Cross explained—The first stop on this second leg of their journey was the Cross at the bottom of the Hill, where Christian lost his burden. Seeing it inspired Christiana to ask Great-heart to explain the meaning of the second part of the statement spoken by the Keeper about forgiveness in both word and deed, for though she had grasped the first part, the second still eluded her somewhat. Happy to oblige, he explained to them that it meant that the Keeper, who was the transmitter of the pardon, had more than enough righteousness to absolve the sins of all who called upon him. Great-heart emphasized that he was of a double nature, at once one with God the Father and also the pure human being chosen to be the mediator between men and God. **The four types of righteousness**—He explained that there were three distinct types of righteousness: the righteousness of the Father, of the Son, and of him who was prepared for the role of mediator. Yet none of these was the righteousness that redeemed. That was reserved for the fourth type: it was his obedience to God's Will that entitled him to this exalted position without equal, just as Adam's disobedience ruined the fate of all mankind. Finally, the Mediator's ultimate sacrifice on the Cross was the means by which he washed away mankind's sins.

Christiana wanted to know whether the other types of righteousness were of any use to them, to which Great-heart replied that they were indeed. They provided the fourth righteousness with its vitality: for the righteousness of God infused the Mediator's obedience with power; his pure human righteousness put him in a position to absolve others; and the righteousness of his position as Mediator gave authority to his obedience. Also, since Christ had such an excess of righteousness that he did not personally need, and since the law of God requires that those who have excess provide for those in need, it stands to reason that Christ should provide for his needy neighbors—and this he does without hesitation.

The repayment of mankind's debt through Christ's sacrifice on the Cross—This, according to Great-heart, was the definition of pardon by deed, but there was another factor needed for its completion. Because the law was based on justice, someone had to repay the debt, or make amends for the transgression. That was the purpose of the Cross—to function as a repayment of our debts and to save us from the full weight of the justice of the law of God. And that was why those who beheld the Cross and understood could shed their burdens, no matter how heavy, and thus feel lighter and happier.

The deep affection and devotion inspired by the Cross—In addition to a greater lightness, the Cross inspired deep affection for Jesus in those who heard the spiritual call. Christiana, who understood this firsthand, waxed eloquent on the subject, wishing that those who had rejected the idea of pilgrimage were there so that they, too, could experience the transformation that it inspired. But Great-heart stressed that this feeling was a special gift of grace—that there were some who had even witnessed the physical Jesus bleeding to death who, instead of weeping, had mocked and laughed, while others were moved to follow him as his disciples.

Simple, Sloth, and Presumption now hang in shackles for their misdeeds—Next they came to where Christian had met with Simple, Sloth, and Presumption, who at the time had been sleeping but were now hanging in irons. Great-heart explained that they not only had the wrong qualities for making a pilgrimage but that they also tried to dissuade others from the Way. They had even succeeded in some cases: the pilgrims Slow-pace, Short-wind, No-heart, Linger-after-Lust, Sleepy-head, and Dull had all been persuaded to quit the Way through negative reports and discouraging untruths about the Lord, the ultimate destination, and the pilgrims who persisted and tried to help others in the process. They were made to feel that their efforts would be pointless and that their goal was nothing but a fairy tale.

The spring at the base of the Hill Difficulty—Finally, they came to the Hill Difficulty, where Great-heart showed them the spring of water where Christian had refreshed himself before ascending the Hill. At the time, the water had been pure. Since then, however, some pilgrims who wanted to prevent others from drinking had muddied it with their feet. According to Great-heart, though, if they placed the water in a pure vessel, it would give it a chance to clarify as the dirt separated and sank.

The false paths now closed off—After the women and children had followed his instructions and refreshed themselves, Great-heart showed them the false paths leading up the Hill, where Formality and Hypocrisy were misled and either maimed or killed. These paths were now clearly closed off by chains, posts, and a ditch, but according to Great-heart, some pilgrims chose to go there anyway, despite warnings from servants of the King.

Ascending the Hill Difficulty—As they made their way up the Hill, Christiana, who had criticized those who were too lazy to take the direct path and chose the byways instead, now found herself panting and wishing for relief. Mercy, too, longed to sit, and the youngest boy started to cry. Great-heart, however, urged them to continue up the path until they reached the Arbor, and in the meantime, he extended his hand to the youngest to help him along.

Rest and refreshment in the Lord's Arbor—Once at the Arbor, they expressed their gratitude to the Lord of the Hill for building such a pleasant resting place, but Mercy, who had heard of Christian's misadventure there, reminded them to avoid falling asleep. When Great-heart asked the boys how they were doing, the youngest thanked him for taking his hand but added that he preferred the difficult uphill climb toward Life to an easy downward path toward Hell and Death. Christiana then offered them some food, which the Interpreter had given her when they departed: some pomegranate, a honeycomb, and something to drink. So they ate and drank and rested, though Great-heart declined the food since he would be returning soon and since they needed the strength for their journey.

The importance of watchfulness—Once the pilgrims had rested and refreshed themselves sufficiently, Great-heart suggested that they move along since the time was already late. Christiana soon noticed that she had left her bottle behind, and as one of her boys went to retrieve it, Mercy inquired about why people seemed to regularly lose things there. Great-heart replied that resting pilgrims often let down their guard and, as a result, either fell asleep or forgot something. It was, therefore, essential to remember to always watch, no matter how pleasant the temporary resting place.

A warning to mind their words and feelings—
Before arriving at the place where the lions were kept, the group of pilgrims came across a platform with verses attached to it that warned people to guard both their speech and feelings. Otherwise, the verses stated, they would end up like those before them (referring to Timorous and Mistrust), who tried to convince Christian to discontinue his pilgrimage and had their tongues seared with a hot iron.

The Giant Grim and the chained lions—As they approached the lions, they were accosted by a giant named Grim, who tried to prevent them from going that way. It was clear, too, from the grassy overgrowth on the King's Highway that he had succeeded in frightening away many other pilgrims. Undeterred, Great-heart drew his sword and struck at the giant until he fell down dead. And so, though still frightened, the women and children went through the narrow passageway and past the chained lions. The boys, who had been leading the group, now walked behind, which prompted a teasing from Great-heart, who asked them whether they only cared to lead when the path seemed safe.

Great-heart delivers the pilgrims to the House Beautiful—When they reached the Porter's Lodge, Great-heart knocked at the door, and on hearing his voice, the Porter recognized it immediately. Great-heart explained how he had brought some pilgrims and that they were late because he had to fight the giant who had been blocking the passageway where the lions were chained. The Porter invited him to spend the night, but Great-heart explained that he had to return to his master's house. Hearing this, the pilgrim's begged him to accompany them for the rest of their journey since they feared they were too weak to withstand all the difficulties by themselves and because they appreciated his caring, strength, and guidance. But Great-heart informed them that their request came too late and that only at the bidding of his Lord could he accompany them the rest of the way. For now, he was obliged to return, and so, he bid them all farewell.

Christiana introduces her group and settles in for the night—Next, Christiana, on being asked the usual questions, informs the Porter of her origin, explaining that she is Christian's widow, now gone on pilgrimage with her children and her friend. Christiana and her party are then brought to the main household, where the household members rejoice at the pilgrims' arrival, offering them rest, dinner, and lodging—at Christiana's request, in the same room where her husband stayed before her. Once alone, Christiana and Mercy discuss how surprised they are that Christiana should be following in Christian's footsteps and is now sleeping in the same bed as he did. Content with their choice to make the pilgrimage and hopeful that they will reach their goal, they fall asleep to the sound of joyful music wafting through the house.

Mercy's dream—The next morning, Christiana asks Mercy what made her laugh in her sleep. Surprised that she had been laughing, Mercy tells her of a dream in which she was lamenting her own hard heart, while others laughed at her and maligned her. Suddenly, she saw a winged person approach, who, when he had come near, comforted her, dressed her in beautiful clothing, and then led her to a glorious place—right up to the throne, where she was welcomed and where she thought she caught a glimpse of Christian. To Christiana, this was a communication from God and a likely sign that Mercy would complete her pilgrimage. With that, Christiana decided that it was time to get up and find out what was in store for them next.

The pilgrims are invited to stay for a longer period—After the women exchanged morning greetings with the household, they were invited to spend at least another month at the house, which they gladly accepted, especially since Mercy had expressed an interest in getting better acquainted with the maidens Charity, Prudence, and Piety.

Prudence questions and instructs the boys—Then Prudence, curious to see how well Christiana had instructed her children, asked whether she could catechize them. Beginning with James, the youngest, she asked him both who made him and who saved him. In both cases, he gave the Trinity as the answer, namely, God in the three forms of Father, Son, and Holy Ghost. Then Prudence asked him how the saving was done in each case, to which he answered that the Father saved by his Grace; the Son by his righteousness, blood, death, and life; and the Holy Ghost through illumination, renovation, and preservation.

Impressed, Prudence decided to ask Joseph, the next youngest, a separate set of questions. First, she asked him to define "man," followed by the word "saved;" then to specify what it meant to be saved by the Trinity; to explain God's reason for saving men; and to tell who would be saved. Joseph willingly answered that man was a creature of reason created by God; that to be saved meant to be brought out of the prison of sin; that only God was capable of this; that the purpose of salvation was for the glory of God and the happiness of mankind; and that those who were saved were those who accepted salvation.

Next, Prudence questioned the next oldest boy, Samuel. After requesting his permission, as was her habit, she asked him to define Heaven and Hell and to explain why going to Heaven was a desirable thing. He answered that Heaven was a state and place of blessedness, where God dwelt; that Hell was the opposite, a miserable state and place characterized by Satan, sin, and death; and that to be in Heaven meant to fully enjoy, in a way not attainable on earth, the presence of God and Christ, the total experience of the Holy Spirit, and the ability to serve and love eternally and tirelessly.

Finally, she came to Matthew, the oldest, whom she asked the following questions: whether anything had existed before God; what he (Matthew) thought of the Bible; whether there were any passages that he did not understand and how he dealt with that; and what he believed in relation to the resurrection of the dead. Matthew replied that God was eternal and that nothing came before Him; that the Bible was the sacred Word of God; that there was much in the Bible that he did not understand and that in such cases, he would pray that the all-wise God would reveal the answers as He saw fit; and finally, that the almighty God had promised (and therefore it must be true) that in the resurrection, the dead would rise with the same physical bodies as before, except that they would be incorruptible.

Prudence's final instructions to the boys: the four sources for learning—Pleased with their answers, Prudence instructed the boys to keep learning from four sources in particular: 1) their mother, who so far had instructed them well; 2) others who were versed in the Way and who had good intentions toward them; 3) the teachings of Nature and Heaven; and 4) the Bible itself.

Mr. Brisk courts Mercy—After about a week's stay, Mercy started being courted by a young man, Mr. Brisk, who pretended to be religious but who was, in fact, a man of the world. Aside from being attractive, Mercy liked to busy herself with sewing projects for the poor. Not knowing the reason for her industry, Mr. Brisk decided that she would make a good housewife and continued setting his eye upon her. Mercy, however, wisely checked with the members of the household to see what she could learn about him, and in the process discovered that he was not as pious as he liked to pretend. Their advice was to keep doing what she was doing. Once he found out that she gave the clothes away, he would change his mind and lose interest. And that was exactly what happened. When Mr. Brisk inquired about Mercy's reasons for her industry, she told him of her love and concern for the poor, after which he decided that, lovely as she was, she had an undesirable "condition." She was not at all disappointed by his loss of interest and resolved that she would rather be married to her "condition" than to unite with someone whose goals in life were at cross-purposes with hers. Furthermore, she had her sister Bountiful's example to strengthen her resolve: her sister also had a heart for the poor, which led her more worldly husband to toss her out of the house. To Mercy and Prudence, it seemed that there were many in those days who professed religion but only few who were willing to practice it.

Matthew's illness from eating the evil fruit and Dr. Skill's cure—Around that time, Christiana's oldest boy, Matthew, grew extremely ill so that Christiana felt it necessary to send for a well-known physician named Mr. Skill. After examining the boy, the doctor concluded that he was suffering from severe, potentially fatal indigestion and inquired as to what he had been eating. Christiana insisted that his diet had been entirely wholesome, but Samuel then reminded her that at the beginning of the trip, Matthew had eaten some of the fruit from the walled garden to the left of the Way. Even when Christiana had scolded him, he had ignored her and kept eating. On hearing this, the physician informed them that that was Beelzebub's garden and that many who had eaten its fruit had died. But he also quickly assured her that Matthew was likely to survive and do well once he was purged. To this end, he concocted a medicine of hyssop, goat's blood, and calf's ashes, but that was too weak. He then created a second cure in pill form from the Body and Blood of Christ (phrased in Latin in the original), combined with salt and a special promise. If the boy would take these three times a day while fasting and repenting, he would be cleansed. At first, Matthew resisted, but then his mother tasted it and described it as being wonderfully sweet, so he finally took the medicine and was cured after purging, sweating, and resting. Impressed, Christiana asked the physician whether the medicine had any other benefits, to which he replied that it was both a cure-all and a preventive medicine, and that taken properly, it could even make a person immortal. But, he cautioned, it must be taken exactly as prescribed—

otherwise, it would be useless. Christiana then requested that he make twelve boxes of the medicine so that she and her group would never have to take regular medication again.

Matthew asks Prudence for instruction—
Following that, Matthew asks Prudence various questions, in response to her promise to the boys to instruct them and answer any questions they might have. The thrust of Prudence's answers is strongly allegorical, indicating that Bunyan sees Nature as an allegory for the workings of divine Law and Grace. For example, Matthew asks why flames rise, while the sun's rays shine down onto the earth. Prudence answers that the flames represent the soul's ascent to God, while the rays stand for God's Grace reaching down toward men. Similarly, Matthew asks about the significance of rain clouds gathering their water from the sea, to which Prudence replies that it symbolizes the minister's knowledge gathered from God: as the clouds rain down upon the earth, so should a minister disperse his knowledge to others. Likewise, the candle, which is thoroughly burned by the flame, signifies the soul in complete service to the Divine.

The pilgrims' final lessons at House Beautiful—
After a month at the house, it was time for the pilgrims to leave, so Joseph reminded his mother, Christiana, to send a request to the Interpreter to have Great-heart accompany them on the rest of their journey. This she did and was fortunate to receive a positive response from the Interpreter. In the meantime, the maidens of House Beautiful wanted to show their valued guests some of the house's additional treasures. First, there was one of Eve's apples, which caused both her own and Adam's downfall. Next, they brought them to Jacob's Ladder, with angels ascending, which caused a stir among Christiana's little group so that they wanted to stay a bit longer in the room. After that, they showed Christiana the Golden Anchor, which they had her take down to bring on the journey so that she could throw it beyond the veil when the time came. Next, they brought them to the mountain and altar where Abraham planned to sacrifice Isaac, which greatly impressed them because of his self-sacrificing reverence and devotion. Finally, Prudence played a song for them on the harpsichord, summarizing all they had just seen.

The pilgrims prepare to leave with Great-heart—
At that point, Great-heart knocked on the door, bringing provisions for the Way from the Interpreter. With Prudence and Piety accompanying them, they made their way to the gate, where they questioned the Porter as to any recent news of pilgrims in the area. He told them that one had gone by some time ago with news of a robbery, though the thieves had been caught since then. Seeing the two women's fear, Matthew reminded his mother that Great-heart's presence would assure their safety. With that, Christiana thanked the Porter deeply, giving him a gold coin as a token of her appreciation for all he had done for them. The Porter, in turn, bowed and blessed them all, wishing them well on their path toward the Divine.

The country birds' special songs—When they had gone a little ways, Piety, who was still with them, suddenly remembered that she had left behind her parting gift for the pilgrims. As she ran back to the house, Christiana noticed some unusual melodic strains coming from a grove to the right. They seemed to be singing praises to God, and as she listened, she heard a response, another hymn of praise to the Divine. When she asked Prudence about it, she was told that they were songs of country birds that only sang on warm, sunny spring days and that their melodies brought cheer wherever they were heard.

Piety presents the pilgrims with a gift—When Piety returned, she presented Christiana with an outline of the treasures they had shown them in the house. Her thought was that they should function as a reminder, guide, and comfort along the Way.

The descent to the Valley—The pilgrims' next stop was the Valley of Humiliation, and though Piety warned them that that was where Christian had battled with Apollyon, Great-heart explained that Christian's difficulties in the Valley had been brought about by the slips he made on his way down the Hill. He explained that the Valley could be as a pleasant and fruitful a place for some as it was difficult for others and that their experience of it was the result of their own actions rather than any innate quality it possessed. After they noticed a pillar that warned them of Christian's slips and his resulting difficulties, Great-heart explained further that it was harder to come down the Hill than to go up. They had already noticed how slippery it was on their way down, but because they had been extremely careful, they were able to avoid any problems.

The Valley of Humiliation and its lesson of exalting the humble—As Great-heart continued describing the Valley, he added that it was the most fertile land in the area, full of green meadows and lilies in the summer. Its lesson was that God lifted up the humble but put down the proud, and so to the humble, it seemed an abundant place. Just as Great-heart was explaining this, they spotted a shepherd boy singing of exactly that theme—of the joys of the humble life, content with little. To such a person, material wealth was a burden, and Great-heart affirmed that only a true pilgrim would love this place. In fact, the Lord himself had once had a country home here because of his love of the area. And despite Christian's difficulties with Apollyon, some had had the opposite experience of meeting angels or finding treasures. Samuel then asked him where Christian had fought with Apollyon, to which Great-heart replied that it had taken place in a dangerous passageway near Forgetful Green, so called because some pilgrims lost sight of the gifts they had already been given. And because of their lack of humility, since they were gifts of grace and not of merit, they ran into hardships. Mercy then added that she felt at ease in the Valley and that she preferred such quiet, empty places to the noise of busier ones. She felt that they gave a person a chance to think about God and the things of the spirit. Great-heart agreed that he often felt well when traveling through it and that others of a humble and devout spirit had said the same.

The site of the battle with Apollyon—At that point, they arrived at the battle area, and Great-heart related the details of the battle to them. He pointed out the remnants of the fight: Christian's bloodstains on the rocks, broken-off pieces from Apollyon's arrows, split stones, and heavy footprints where they stamped their feet. There was even a statue commemorating both the battle and Christian's triumph.

The Valley of the Shadow of Death—Next they came to the Valley of the Shadow of Death, which was fraught with many frightening and evil things, though having Great-heart lead them while it was still light made the passage considerably easier. There were sounds of groaning and hissing; at one point, the ground under their feet shook; and they were almost accosted by a fiend, though it disappeared once it neared Great-heart. When little James started feeling ill, Christiana fed him some of Mr. Skill's cure-all pills, and he improved. Then Mercy noticed a roaring lion running toward them, but like the fiend, it backed off on approaching Great-heart and sensing that there would be a fight.

The hellish pit amidst darkness and mist—Next, they came to a great pit, and just then, they found themselves enveloped in darkness and mist so that they were at a loss as to what to do. Great-heart, undaunted as always, told them to wait, that this, too, would be solved. While they stood there, they clearly perceived the smoke, fire, and demonic rushing noises and sensations emanating from the pit. Thinking of the trials her husband must have undergone, Christiana felt deeply moved. Though she had heard the horrible stories, they paled in the face of the reality.

The prayer for Divine aid is answered—Great-heart likened it to traveling in rough seas but assured the group of pilgrims that he had gone through there many times, often in much more difficult circumstances, and that if they trusted and prayed for God's power and light, they would make it safely through. On doing this, they received the light and help they needed, and though they had to deal with the offensive stench of the place, Samuel reminded them all that to pass through there was not nearly as bad as having to stay for eternity. After all, their trials would make their final reward seem that much better. Hearing this, Great-heart applauded the boy for speaking like a man.

The snares and the ditch—Great-heart next warned them to be careful where they stepped, since they were surrounded by snares. He showed them one man, Heedless, who by not paying attention had been caught in a snare, fallen into the ditch, and been torn to pieces. His friend, Takeheed, had done better, though many others had died. Their mistake was that they lacked the necessary seriousness and neglected to find a guide to help them. He marveled that Christian had done so well, which he attributed to both God's special love for him and Christian's own benevolent heart.

The Giant Maul by the cave—Following that, they came to a cave inhabited by one Maul, a giant who tried to distract young pilgrims from the Way with his false teachings. He was determined to prevent Great-heart from escorting any more women and children out of his own Lord's kingdom, and so the two fought a bitter fight. At one point, while they were both resting, Great-heart busied himself with prayer. When the fight resumed, the giant almost overcame him, but Great-heart finally chopped off his head, afterwards constructing a pillar to tell the story to future pilgrims. A little further along, they rested and nourished themselves, while Christiana asked Great-heart how he had felt during the battle. From his answers, it was clear that he placed his entire faith in God, a notion that was supported by Matthew, the oldest boy, when he added that God's acts of grace and deliverance toward them had been so plentiful that they no longer had any reason to doubt.

Great-heart finds Old Honest sleeping by the roadside—Next, they came to an oak tree, where they saw an old pilgrim sleeping. When Great-heart woke him, the old man started suddenly, questioning who they were. After reassuring him, Great-heart introduced himself and his group and told the elderly pilgrim of their purpose to go to the Celestial City. The man explained he had been worried that they were thieves, like the ones who had troubled Little-Faith, but he saw now that they were honest folk. When Great-heart asked him what he would have done if they had, in fact, been thieves, he insisted that he would have fought with all he had and that anyone who thought otherwise of a pilgrim, did not understand the nature of a true Christian. After speaking a bit further together, they discovered that the old pilgrim's name was Honest and that he was from the town called Stupidity. Great-heart marveled that he should be from there, since that town had an even worse reputation than the City of Destruction. Honest agreed with him but also affirmed that when the light of God, which he called the "Sun of Righteousness," shone on a person's heart, it could pierce through any frigidity or dullness.

Honest rejoices at meeting Christiana and her group—Next, the other pilgrims introduced themselves, and when Honest learned who Christiana was, he jumped for joy, having heard so much about Christian. Then he blessed each of the children and Mercy in turn, according to their names, urging them to be like their Biblical counterparts or, in Mercy's case, like the quality her name represented.

Great-heart tells the story of Mr. Fearing and his deep sense of unworthiness—Curious, Great-heart inquired whether Honest was familiar with Mr. Fearing, who was from the same area. Honest replied that he knew him well but had found him problematic because of all his fears, even though he had the right basic characteristics to be a pilgrim.

From the Slough to the Interpreter's House—Great-heart then explained that he had escorted Mr. Fearing from the Interpreter's house all the way to the Celestial Gate. He noticed during that time that Fearing was afraid of being inadequate and unworthy. There had been talk that he lay stuck in the Slough of Despond for more than a month, even refusing multiple offers for help from passersby. Eventually, he broke out of the Slough and moved on, though not from his state of despondency. When he arrived at the Wicket Gate, he stood there for a long time, watching many others go in ahead of him before he finally knocked. When the gate was opened, and the Gatekeeper questioned him, he fell down trembling and had to be encouraged and invited in to come in. He suffered from ongoing feelings of shame and unworthiness, even once inside the house.

Great-heart finds Fearing outside in the cold and coaxes him indoors—The same sort of thing happened at the Interpreter's house, where Great-heart met him. He stayed outside in the cold before mustering the courage to ask for admittance, despite the fact that he had been given a special note requesting a protective escort for the remainder of the Way. Again, he watched as others knocked and went in before him. At last, when he was on the brink of starvation, Great-heart happened to look outside and spotted him by the door. When he opened it to find out what he wanted, he noticed that he was crying and quickly figured out what was going on. After consulting with his master and the household, he went back out and, following a great deal of effort, he finally convinced the man to come in. There, he was treated with exceptional tenderness and care by the Lord of the house, who was deeply merciful and kind, and after the man had gained some courage and comfort and seen the different rooms in the house, the Interpreter sent him on his way with food and drink, accompanied by Great-heart.

Great-heart escorts Fearing to the House Beautiful—As they set out on their way, Great-heart observed that the man sighed a great deal. On seeing the three hanged men by the Way, Fearing expressed concern that he would meet with the same fate. The Cross and the Sepulchre had a positive effect on him, and the Hill and the Lions seemed not to bother him—it was only his sense of unworthiness that was his great burden.

Fearing at the House Beautiful—At the House Beautiful on the Hill, he seemed too shy to converse with the household members, though he loved to secretly listen to them talk. In fact, he had loved being at the Gatekeeper's and Interpreter's houses, but his shyness had made it difficult for him to express himself.

Fearing's ease descending the Hill and his love of the Valley of the Humiliation—Back on the Way, he had no problem going down the Hill and seemed particularly suited to the Valley of Humiliation, where he was happier than anywhere else, rising early to walk and enjoy the earth and flowers, which he would hug and kiss.

A quiet passage through the Valley of the Shadow of Death—Once they reached the Valley of the Shadow of Death, however, it was a different story. His initial fear, which gripped him terribly, was that the hobgoblins would take him. But as they passed through the Valley, Great-heart observed that it was unusually quiet, which made him think that the Lord of the Way had made special arrangements to silence its inhabitants in order to ease the way for Mr. Fearing.

Great-heart escorts Fearing all the way to the Celestial Gate—Great-heart recounted just a few more things about Fearing's journey: how he had railed so much against the people at Vanity Fair that Great-heart feared being taken down by them; and how he had remained watchful and awake during their trek through the Enchanted Ground. At the river, he became fearful again, but Great-heart noticed that the water was lower than he had ever seen it, and so, Fearing eventually made it over and arrived at the Celestial Gate, where they parted ways.

Fearing's profound sensitivity and goodness—Great-heart never doubted that Fearing would be accepted, and even Fearing seemed confident when they separated. For Great-heart had noticed that he had a deeply sensitive spirit and was especially disturbed by sin, often preferring others to himself for fear of hurting them in some way—even when he was entitled to whatever he denied himself.

Two reasons for despondency—It seemed strange to Honest that such a good man should be in such a depressed state throughout his life. Great-heart explained first, that God created two types of dispositions—the cheerful and the melancholy; and second, that when readjusting the human soul from a state of sinfulness, He sends a state of despondency before bringing it into a condition of happiness and harmony. The difference with Mr. Fearing was that his suffering lasted till almost the end of his journey, and he seemed capable of little else.

The other pilgrims compare their own experiences to Mr. Fearing's—After Great-heart was done with Mr. Fearing's story, Christiana mentioned that she had similar fears but that they had a different effect on her. Instead of expressing them, like Fearing, she kept quiet about them, and instead of being afraid to knock at the doors of the various houses, she knocked even more loudly for fear that she would be rejected. Mercy also related to his priorities—his utter lack of fear in relation to worldly trials compared to his total fear of rejection at the heavenly Gate. Little James added that the one fear worth entertaining was the fear of God, to which Great-heart added that it was indeed the beginning of true wisdom. Having said all there was to say about Mr. Fearing's journey to the Celestial Gate, Great-heart finished with a song applauding Fearing's reverence and devotion to God and hoping that others would learn from him.

Honest tells of Mr. Self-will's beliefs—Next, Mr. Honest told them about another companion of his, Mr. Self-will. His distinguishing characteristic was that he did what he wanted rather than obeying the Divine laws or the advice or example of others. Honest even tried speaking with him several times, but it was of no use. Self-will's concept of Salvation was that vice and virtue were equal and that if a man practiced both, he was assured of Salvation. His argument was that if the best of God's people were guilty of various sins, then he, too, could participate in them. That meant that, like key Biblical figures such as David, Solomon, and Sarah, he could lie, cheat, steal, and commit adultery and polygamy. The only prerequisite for such behavior was that the person possess the same merits as the Biblical examples. Great-heart likened this to a dog eating a child's feces in the belief that it would become like the child, noting that people with such beliefs were only seeking excuses to do as they pleased. Honest added that there were many who thought like him but who kept their opinions private. In spite of their beliefs, they dared to make the pilgrimage, but as Great-heart said, they would all be outpaced by the true pilgrims. Honest, who had been a pilgrim for many years, told of the many different kinds of pilgrims he had seen and how they fared long-term. Some that at first seemed unlikely to last proved surprisingly able, persisting to the end, while others that seemed more enthusiastic or capable, either changed their minds or died along the Way.

The group is warned against thieves—Suddenly, they noticed a man coming toward them in a rush, who when he came near, warned them to guard themselves against the thieves who had assaulted Little-Faith. But Great-heart, unperturbed by the news, simply said that they were prepared to deal with them and kept moving, together with the rest of the pilgrims. Interestingly, the thieves never showed.

Honest leads them to Gaius' Inn—At that point, Christiana and the children were tired, so she requested that they find an inn. Honest happened to know of one in the area, which luckily was owned by one Gaius, who kept it especially for pilgrims. After Gaius showed them to their rooms, Great-heart inquired about supper, promising to be content with whatever they had.

Gaius meets his guests—As the cook Taste-that-which-is-Good was preparing the meal, Gaius asked his guest's names. By then, Christiana appears to have aged, since he referred to her as "this aged matron," implying that a significant amount of time has passed since the pilgrims' journey first began. Excited to discover that she was Christian's wife, Gaius told them about Christian's forefathers, a lineage of strong, virtuous men that went back to such apostles and martyrs as Stephen, James, Peter, and Paul. When Great-heart mentioned that Christian's sons were as enthusiastic about the Way as their father and forefathers had been, Gaius strongly recommended that Christiana find wives for the boys—who had grown up by now—so that the lineage could continue and spread. He even suggested that Mercy and Matthew be married, which Christiana promptly arranged.

Gaius praises women—Then Gaius launched into a defense of women, who had acquired a bad name through Eve's original sin of eating the apple from the Tree of the Knowledge of Good and Evil. He says that it was also through a woman that the Savior of the world was born, and women had been faithful in following and serving Christ, even being the first to see him after his Resurrection and to report the vision to the disciples, who did not at first believe. He therefore concluded that women must also be partakers of the Grace that had been bestowed on men.

A symbolic meal—About that time, the hosts started to set the table for dinner, which made Matthew feel hungrier than before. That inspired Gaius to launch into a metaphor about the even greater desirability of the Lord's Supper and that all preachings and other reminders should serve to whet his appetite. Soon the dinner arrived, which consisted of various courses, most with religious symbolism. First, there were the wave-shoulder and heave offering, which symbolized David's offering to God. Then there was a bottle of wine, which stood for the True Vine. Next they brought a dish of milk for the boys' growth, followed by butter and honey—reputedly the Savior's childhood food—for wisdom and comfort. After that, they set some apples on the table, which prompted Matthew to ask whether apples were permitted, since an apple was the instrument that the serpent had used to deceive Eve and since he himself had become sick from eating forbidden fruit. Gaius reassured him that although apples symbolized the forbidden fruit, they were also the symbol of spiritual Love. Finally, they brought a bowl of nuts, which, when some expressed concern over damage to the children's teeth, Gaius turned the statement into a proverb. He compared the nuts to difficult spiritual texts that, once cracked, yielded meat but until then remained impossible to access.

The power of generosity—After many hours of cheerful conversation, Honest asked Gaius to solve a riddle about a man who, though he perpetually gave away what he had, continued to increase. After some thought, Gaius answered that those who gave to the poor would receive far more in return. When Joseph expressed his amazement at Gaius' ability, the innkeeper said that he had learned the truth of this law from experience—that giving tended to make rich, though not necessarily materially, while greed and stinginess tended toward poverty.

Gaius and his guests converse all night—After Gaius had shown the tired boys to their room, he returned to converse with his guests for a long while, so much did he and his guests enjoy each others' company. At one point, the conversation centered on 1) the importance of Divine Grace as the essential cleansing and freeing element in the soul's journey and 2) how a person who wanted to truly live had to first die to himself. People should also not confuse an easier path with superior attainment, since the more obstacles a person had, the greater the potential attainment. The relative calm of old age should not, for example, be mistaken for a higher spiritual peace.

Great-heart kills the Giant Slay-good and frees Feeble-mind—The next day, Gaius suggested that since Great-heart was so skilled with weapons, they pay a visit to a man-eating giant, Slay-good, who headed a band of thieves and had been causing trouble for pilgrims along the Highway. Perhaps they could help out future pilgrims by eliminating this problem. When they approached the giant, they saw that he had gotten hold of a man named Feeble-mind, from the town of Uncertain, and was searching his clothes before eating him. When the giant asked them what they wanted, Great-heart told him that they had come to avenge the pilgrims he had slain. After a challenging fight, Great-heart finally chopped off the giant's head and brought it to the inn to display as a warning to would-be troublemakers.

Feeble-mind—Feeble-mind also came with Great-heart to the inn, where he told the pilgrims his story. Being weak-minded and sickly, he had despaired of ever achieving wellness in his hometown, so he set out on a pilgrimage. He found himself welcomed and kindly entertained at the different houses along the Way, and many pilgrims temporarily slowed their pace to help. One of the servants from the Interpreter's house even carried him up the Hill of Difficulty, since it was judged too strenuous a climb for him. His encounter with the giant was too much for him to handle by himself, but in spite of being robbed and held hostage, he never lost faith that all would be well, and he thanked both his Lord and those who rescued him. For one thing in his life was certain: though his mind and body were weak, his faith was strong.

The convertible nature of good and evil circumstances—Honest inquired whether he knew Mr. Fearing, to which Feeble-mind replied that Fearing was his uncle, that he knew him well and was aware of their similarities. Gaius then extended his full hospitality to Feeble-mind, prompting his new guest to proclaim how even evil occurrences could fulfill the plan of goodness. Just as he was saying this, a messenger arrived with the urgent news that a pilgrim named Not-right had been struck dead by lightning along the Way. Recognizing him as someone who sought his company but then fled during the fray with the giant, Feeble-mind once more exclaimed that this was another instance of how good circumstances could turn into evil ones and vice versa.

The pilgrims stay on at the inn and two of the sons, now grown, are married—Impressed by Gaius' goodness, Samuel had previously asked to stay on at the inn for a while, which Gaius' willingly granted, and while they were there, both Mercy and Matthew as well as James and Phebe, Gaius' daughter, were married.

Gaius refuses to charge the pilgrims for room and board—Eventually, it came time for the pilgrims to leave, and when they had feasted and enjoyed themselves according to Gaius' gracious hospitality, Great-heart asked for the bill. Gaius, however, declined his offer, explaining that he boarded pilgrims for free and that his payment came from the Good Samaritan, who promised to cover all expenses on his return to the inn. Hearing that, Great-heart blessed him for his generosity, and they all said goodbye to one another.

Feeble-mind hesitates to join the pilgrims for fear of slowing them down—As they were leaving, Great-heart noticed that Feeble-mind hesitated, so he urged him to come along, assuring him that he would be his guide and provide him safe conduct. Feeble-mind, however, resisted, feeling that he would be a burden on the others because of his weak mental, emotional, and physical condition. He did not feel that he would be able to keep pace or to enjoy the things that others normally enjoyed. Also, being a weak Christian, he felt that he would be offended by things that didn't bother his stronger brothers and sisters.

The commitment of the strong to care for the weak and the arrival of Ready-to-halt—To this, Great-heart replied that he had a duty to care for his weaker brethren and that he and the other pilgrims would be happy to slow their pace and forgo their own comforts and pleasures for his sake. Just then, a lame man on crutches, whose name was Mr. Ready-to-halt, happened to be passing by the inn on his pilgrimage. Seeing him, Feeble-mind welcomed him, exclaiming that he had appeared at exactly the right time, as he was wishing for appropriate company for his journey. Happy to oblige, Ready-to-halt joined the party, taking up the rear with Feeble-mind as the rest went on ahead, with Great-heart and Honest leading.

The pilgrims arrive in Vanity and stay with Mr. Mnason—As they were walking, Honest asked Great-heart to recount some of the tales of earlier pilgrims, so Great-heart began with a quick retelling of the adventures of Christian and Faithful, describing them as determined, "lion-like" men. By evening, they had arrived at the town of Vanity, where Great-heart knew an elderly disciple from Cyprus named Mr. Mnason. So they proceeded to his house, and recognizing Great-heart's voice, Mnason opened the door and welcomed them.

Mnason fetches some of the few good people in Vanity to meet his guests—After Mnason showed them to their rooms and into the dining area, Honest asked him whether there were any good folk in the town and if they could spend some time with them to refresh their souls. Mnason replied that there were a few and sent his daughter Grace to fetch them. Their names were Contrite, Holy-man, Love-saint, Dare-not-lie, and Penitent, and they all came quickly in response. When they discovered who Christiana was, they were all amazed and blessed the boys, wishing upon them the same Grace that their father had received.

Improvement of the town since Faithful's martyrdom—Honest asked about the town's current attitudes and was told that, since Faithful's death, the town had become more moderate, though fair season was still a difficult time for religious people, who needed a means of remembrance to maintain their watchfulness. But in general, the town had a more favorable attitude toward religion, especially in some areas. He guessed that their behavior toward Faithful weighed heavily upon their consciences, for since then, there had been no further burnings.

The pilgrims tell how their journey has been so far—Mr. Contrite then asked how their pilgrimage had gone so far and what sort of reception they had had. Honest told him that their journey had been like that of any traveling man—sometimes difficult, sometimes easier—and that they had already met with some dangerous encounters and scuffles. When asked for particulars, Great-heart recounted the women's and children's troubles with the rapists at the beginning of their trip and later, the men's battles with three different giants, one of whom had kidnapped Feeble-mind. He added that they had gone looking for the most recent giant to reduce potential trouble for future pilgrims and that they had displayed his head by the wayside to warn other evildoers.

Required qualities for a true pilgrim—Mr. Holy-man noted that pilgrims needed two things: courage and a pure, blameless life. Without courage, they would be unable to complete their journey; and without blamelessness, they would give other pilgrims a bad reputation. Love-saint and Dare-not-lie added that there were many hypocrites who did not possess either the true pilgrim's spirit or life and who were a discredit to the Master of the Way. But, added Penitent, such so-called pilgrims were not likely to receive the gift of Grace that made it possible to fulfill the goal.

The long stay with Mr. Mnason and the marriage of Christiana's two other sons—The pilgrim party remained a long time with Mr. Mnason in Vanity, and during that time, Grace and Samuel were married as well as Martha, Mnason's other daughter, and Joseph. The young women, especially Mercy, did much good and also bore many children, thereby continuing Christian's good lineage.

Vanquishing the beast—During the pilgrims' stay, Vanity was attacked by a strange and horrifying monster, a dragon-like creature with seven heads and ten horns. And this monster would periodically attack the town, killing people and kidnapping children. Whoever wanted to live had to agree to its terms, which was how it brought the town under its sway.[2] So Great-Heart, along with the other able fighters, Contrite, Holy-man, Dare-not-lie, and Penitent, set out to destroy this beast and managed to injure it so badly that it retreated into the woods. Whenever it returned, they would attack it again, until it became lame and so sorely wounded that it was expected to eventually die, and after a while, the attacks and kidnappings ceased. These brave attacks on the beast gave the pilgrims a favorable reputation in the town, although some of the townsfolk were so depraved that they were unable to appreciate anything beyond their own ways.

---

[2] This and the previous sentence are a reference to Revelation 13.

The pilgrims continue their journey—At last, it came time for the pilgrims to move on, and so they prayed for their protection and were given adequate supplies suitable for all members of their group, both strong and weak, male and female, young and old. Once again, Great-heart led the group, with the weaker men, women, and children walking behind. By this time, as mentioned earlier, Christiana's own children were grown and married, so the children referred to here are her grandchildren, which becomes clear later in the text.

Commemorating Faithful and staying on the path—Their first stop was the site of Faithful's burning, where they paused to do reverence to his valiant and faithful self-sacrifice, which they now realized had made their own pilgrimage far easier. Next, they passed the hill Lucre and the Pillar of Salt, noting that it was a warning to stay on a virtuous path and to avoid foolish and dangerous temptations.

The River of the Water of Life and the Good Shepherd—After that, they came to the river near the Delectable Mountains, to a green area full of trees and meadows. By this river, there were sheepcotes and the house of the compassionate Shepherd, another reference to Christ. Because of this Shepherd's kindness, wisdom, and faithfulness to his sheep, Christiana instructed her daughters-in-law to leave their own children in his care. Aside from the fact that they would want for nothing, this was also a beautiful, fertile area where their children would be guided correctly and protected from harm.

The destruction of Giant Despair and his Castle—
Eventually, they came to By-Path Meadow and the stile, and knowing that this was the place that led to Christian and Hopeful's imprisonment in Doubting Castle, they discussed whether to try destroying Giant Despair and his castle and releasing any prisoners. Great-heart concluded that although there was some question as to the lawfulness of treading on unhallowed ground, he had a mission to destroy evil—and especially doubt and despair—through Faith in the Divine good. Accompanied by Honest and Christiana's four sons, all of them now strong, young men, Great-heart set out on his mission. Once at the castle gate, he knocked loudly, which brought both the giant and his wife to the door. When asked who he was, Great-heart introduced himself and gave a clear report of both his function as a guide for pilgrims and his mission to destroy the giant and his castle. Unperturbed because of his large size and his previous conquests, which included even fallen angels, the giant, armed with a steel helmet, a fiery breast-plate, iron shoes, and a club, exited the castle to meet with Great-heart in battle. His wife, Diffidence, who tried to help, was instantly killed by Honest, and though Giant Despair himself put up a great fight, he was no match for the men and especially for Great-heart, who finally chopped off his head.

The rescue of Mr. Despondency and his daughter Much-afraid—After killing the giant and his wife, the men spent seven days destroying Doubting Castle, where, among the strewn bones of dead men, they found one almost starved man, Mr. Despondency, and his daughter Much-afraid. These they took back with them to the Way, where Christiana supplied Mr. Despondency with food and drink, and Ready-to-halt danced with Much-afraid (despite having to hobble on one crutch) to the music played by Christiana and Mercy on the viol and lute. Great-heart then posted the giant's head by the highway, along with a marble engraving telling of his victory for the encouragement and release of those who still harbored doubts.

The Delectable Mountains and the Shepherds—The pilgrims' next stop was the Delectable Mountains, where they were welcomed by the Shepherds, who marveled at the size of their group. After Great-heart introduced everyone, the Shepherds made a special effort to invite in those who were weak, calling each by name so that they knew that they, too, were welcome. This section stresses the inclusive nature of Christianity, with its insistence that weakness and infirmity should never be a stumbling block to those wanting to enter the kingdom and that the strong had a duty to help the weak. In this spirit, the Shepherds prepared tasty and nourishing food that the weaker pilgrims could digest.

The usual lessons and Mount Marvel—After a good night's sleep, the Shepherds showed the pilgrims the same places they had shown Christian and Hopeful. Following that, they pointed them toward Mount Marvel, where they saw a man moving the hills through the power of his word alone. They told the pilgrims that he was the son of Great Grace, a man whom Great-heart knew and admired, and that he was there to demonstrate the power of Faith.

Mount Innocent and Godly-man—Next, they showed them Mount Innocent, where a man named Godly-man, dressed completely in white, was having his clothes dirtied by two men called Prejudice and Ill-will. But Godly-man's innocence was such that the dirt would not stick to his clothing, proof that a truly innocent life was like a pure, shining light.

Mount Charity and the Two Fools—Their next stop was Mount Charity, where a man was cutting clothes from an unlimited roll of cloth, which, no matter how much he gave away to the poor, never decreased. This, according to the Shepherds, was the spiritual law that said that those with the will to give to the needy would never be in need themselves. After that, they passed two men, Fool and Want-wit, who were trying to make the skin of a black man white by washing him, a metaphor for the impossibility of restoring the reputation of a hypocrite.

The By-way to Hell—Then Mercy asked if she could view the door in the Hill leading to Hell. When the Shepherds brought the pilgrims there, Mercy listened by the door to the curses and moaning—laments that the different individuals wished they had done better rather than be consigned to such torture as they suffered now. After the earth shook beneath her feet as though it, too, was afraid, Mercy turned pale and left, proclaiming that whoever escaped that place was indeed blessed.

Mercy asks for the special Mirror—When they returned to the castle, Mercy found herself yearning for a large mirror she had seen hanging in the dining room. Being pregnant, she felt that she would miscarry if she did not have the mirror, but she was too ashamed to ask the Shepherds. Christiana, seeing her distress, asked her what was wrong, and when she discovered the problem, she assured her that it was a good thing to long for and that there was no need for shame. For Mercy's sake, Christiana would ask the Shepherds if they could buy it from them.

The mirror that Mercy longed for was no ordinary mirror but one that gave two views—one of the person's own features and one of the form and face of Christ, who would appear differently at different times. Some had even seen the holes in his body, hands, and feet or the crown of thorns, while at other times, he appeared in a state of glory. When the Shepherds heard of Mercy's request, they told Christiana to call her, and when she told them what she desired, one of them ran to get it and joyfully delivered it to her. They were likewise generous with the others, giving the young women gifts and adorning them and Christiana with jewels as well as complimenting the young men on their bravery in the face of Giant Despair.

The pilgrims move on—Eventually, it came time for the pilgrims to leave. Bunyan points out here that this group was much better off than the previous pilgrims because they had such an able and experienced guide in Great-heart. For that reason, the Shepherds, whose names were Watchful, Knowledge, Experience, and Sincere, felt no need to equip them with warnings for the Way. The pilgrims thus left, singing with joy that they had been so well received and cared for.

Next, the pilgrims came to where Christian had encountered the rebellious Turn-away, who was so stubborn that no efforts could dissuade him from returning to his home city of Apostasy, even by Evangelist and another who tried to get him to look at the Cross and Sepulchre.

The pilgrims meet Valiant-for-truth—After that, as they were passing the area where Little-Faith had been attacked, they noticed a severely wounded, bloody-faced man holding a sword in his hand. On questioning him, Great-heart discovered that his name was Valiant-for-truth and that he had been attacked by three men named Wild-head, Pragmatick, and Inconsiderate. They had first tried to bully him by giving him the choice of either joining them, returning to his home town, or dying. After citing his reasons for refusing all their choices, he battled them for three hours until they finally fled, probably, he guessed, because they heard Great-heart and the others coming. Impressed with his valor, Great-heart asked him why he had not called for help, to which Valiant-for-truth replied that he had called upon the Lord and that that was enough for him. When Great-heart examined his sword, he found that it was a Jerusalem sword, an all-powerful, indestructible sword that could cut not only flesh and bones but soul and spirit as well. Great-heart then invited him to join their party, being especially pleased to find someone with such courage, stamina, and persistence. And so, having nourished him and cleansed his wounds, they continued on their way.

Valiant-for-truth ignores all resistance to his pilgrimage—On further questioning, Great-heart discovered that Valiant-for-truth was from the city of Dark-Land, on the same coast as the City of Destruction. He had first heard of Christian's story when a person named Tell-true visited their area and told them of Christian's pilgrimage. That inspired Valiant-for-truth so much that he determined to make the pilgrimage himself, despite his parents' protests and arguments to the contrary, which included practically every detail of Christian's trip, with the one error that they claimed he had drowned in the river that had no bridge. Valiant-for-truth, however, chose to listen to Tell-true's account instead of theirs, and he also wisely took Tell-true's advice to enter in at the Wicket Gate, since otherwise his journey would be wasted.

When Great-heart introduced Valiant-for-truth to Christiana and her sons, Valiant-for-truth marveled and rejoiced that Christian's family, who at first rejected him, would now be meeting him in the Celestial City. But he also took the opportunity to ask Great-heart whether he thought people would recognize each other once in that state. Great-heart's reply was that if they knew themselves, why would they not know others, even though the relationship as it was on earth would no longer exist.

Valiant-for-truth's great Faith—Having questioned Valiant-for-truth copiously about his reasons and determination for embarking on his pilgrimage, despite all resistance and difficulties, Great-heart concluded that Valiant-for-truth's greatest strength was his faith. Valiant, agreeing, sang a song that said that he who had the true Faith of Spirit could never be vanquished or frightened off the path and that such Faith would carry him through to the end, when he would inherit eternal Life.

The Enchanted Ground—When the pilgrims entered the Enchanted Ground, they took special care, since they knew that it was a dangerous place. As usual, Great-heart led the group, and for the time being, Valiant-for-truth guarded the rear, while all the other fighting men kept their swords out. Great-heart and Valiant also took special care to encourage and watch out for the weaker members of the group.

The pilgrims avoid the enchanted Arbor called The Slothful's Friend—As they were walking, a dark mist covered the area so that they had to keep contact with each other through speech. The ground was also difficult to walk on, full of dirt, mud, thorns, and thickets, nor were there any places to stop, such as inns or pubs. As they passed a particularly beautiful arbor called The Slothful's Friend, complete with benches and couches to rest on, not one of them made a move to stop there, though they were all tired from their journey. Instead they listened to Great-heart, who warned them that the arbors in this area were dangerous places where, if a pilgrim fell asleep, there was a risk of death.

Great-heart's map prevents them from going astray in the dark and falling into the pit—Next, they came to a fork in the road, and since it was still dark, it was impossible to see that at the end of the easier-looking path, there was a muddy pit that would have trapped and drowned the pilgrims if they had gone in that direction. Luckily, Great-heart always brought his map and a box of sturdy matches, and after studying the map, he determined that the group should go right.

The sleeping pilgrims, Heedless and Too-bold—As they passed another arbor, they noticed two men, Heedless and Too-bold, sleeping, so they tried to wake them without themselves succumbing to the arbor's temptations. When Great-heart finally shook them, they reacted by talking in their sleep, one about money and the other about fighting. Great-heart explained that this sort of thing often happened to the heedless who embarked on pilgrimage, and that was why the Enchanted Ground was placed so near to the Way's end. The idea was to tempt pilgrims when they were most tired from their long journey, so unless travelers had prepared their hearts and minds, they were likely to fall here.

Disturbed by the sight, the pilgrims kept moving, and at their request, Great-heart lit a lantern to ease their way in the darkness. Then the children, who had grown extremely tired, urgently prayed to the Lord of the Way to make things easier for them, and with that, a wind cleared out the fog, improving their visibility.

The pilgrims encounter Standfast praying for deliverance—Near the end of the Enchanted Ground, the pilgrims thought they heard a sound, and just ahead of them on the Way, they noticed a man praying on his knees. When he arose and started running toward the Celestial Gate, Great-heart called after him to stop and join them. On coming nearer, Honest recognized him as being from his own city, and the other, named Standfast, recognized Honest as well. Since they were both honest and committed pilgrims, they were glad to see other, and Honest then inquired about the reason for Standfast's urgent prayer.

Standfast resists the temptations of Madam Bubble—Standfast replied that he was praying for deliverance from the deadly temptations of the Enchanted Ground, which lured pilgrims to sleep unawares. In fact, just as the pilgrim party had arrived, he had been freed from the efforts of an elderly enchantress to tempt him, first, with her body, money, and a bed, and second, with the splendor and happiness of this world. He explained that she was Madam Bubble, mistress of the world, and she tempted him repeatedly, yet he resisted each time even though he was tired and poor. By the time the pilgrims came by, she had just left, so his prayer had turned into one of gratitude to the Lord of the Way.

Honest realized that he, too, had either read about her or seen her in a picture, and he proceeded to describe her perfectly. Great-heart then explained that the ground there was enchanted because of her witchcraft and that many had gone astray by yielding to her worldly temptations and believing her lies. But to yield to her was the road to hell and destruction, despite her promises. He finished by commending Standfast on his steadfastness.

The Land of Beulah—Finally, they came to Beulah, the land of perpetual light and abundant vineyards and orchards, whose fruit was freely available to all pilgrims. The area was owned by the King of the Celestial Country and was thus frequented by both pilgrims and Shining Ones, who came to welcome the travelers after their long journey. Here the pilgrims rested to the extent they could, given that the celestial bells were continuously ringing and the trumpets sounding their heavenly melodies. In spite of this, they found themselves well rested. Here, too, everything was delightful. Only the river's waters were bitter, but then only upon first swallowing. That river changed its flow for different pilgrims, being sometimes high and sometimes low.

Christiana receives the call to proceed to the Celestial City—Soon a pressing message came for Christiana, telling her that she would be the first to cross the River and that she was expected by her Lord and Master within the next ten days. To prove the truth of his message, the messenger gave her an arrow of Love that would transform her heart. So Christiana made her final preparations, gave her parting blessings and admonitions to her children and the other pilgrims, and left what goods she still had to the poor.

The day of her crossing, many came out on both sides of the River—on the one, to bid her farewell, and on the other, to welcome and escort her to the Celestial City. As she entered the waters, she spoke her final words announcing that she was coming to meet her Lord, who received her with the same joyful festivities reserved for all true pilgrims.

Mr. Ready-to-halt receives the call—Next, Mr. Ready-to-halt was called, with a special message given to him to prove the truth of the call. Having been told that his golden bowl had been broken and his silver cord loosed[3], Ready-to-halt said his goodbyes and left his crutches to his son, since he could see that there were chariots and horses waiting for him. As he entered the River, his final words were, "Welcome Life."

---

[3] The first reference to Ecclesiastes 12. Following this, every pilgrim who is called to the Celestial Gate receives a

Mr. Feeble-mind receives the call—Next came Mr. Feeble-mind, who was told that his time had come to see the brightness of his Lord's face firsthand. The message given him was that those who looked through windows would grow dim. After informing his friends, having nothing else to leave behind, he asked Valiant-for-truth to bury his feeble mind in a heap of dung. When he entered the River, he called out for Faith and Patience, and so crossed over.

Mr. Despondency receives the call, and his daughter Much-afraid chooses to go with him—When Mr. Despondency's turn came, his daughter Much-afraid decided to go with him. His token of truth was the burden of a grasshopper. Having nothing to else to leave behind, he and his daughter left their fears and depression; and though they could never rid themselves of them while on earth, they instructed the other pilgrims to bar them entry. As they entered the River, he bid the night farewell and greeted the day, while his daughter sang.

---

message that is a quote from the same chapter, which has to do with the severing of the ties to material existence.

Old Honest receives the call—Next was old Mr. Honest, who was given a week to prepare, with the message that his daughters of music would be humbled. Unlike the others, he left nothing behind but took his honesty along. That day, the waters were high, but his friend Good-Conscience helped him across, as Honesty had previously requested. His final words before crossing were: "Grace Reigns."

Mr. Valiant-for-truth receives the call—Mr. Valiant-for truth was next. His token was that "his pitcher was broken at the fountain." Valiant bequeathed his sword to whoever would follow in his footsteps on a pilgrimage, and he gave his bravery and skill to the one who could take them up. But it was his desire was to bring his scars as proof of the courageous battles he fought in his Lord's name. He entered the River quoting St. Paul in Corinthians 15: "Death, where is thy sting? Grave, where is thy victory?" Many watched him go that day, and the sound of many trumpets met him on the other shore.

Mr. Standfast receives the call—Finally, Mr. Standfast was called. His token message was that his wheel was broken at the cistern. On hearing the news, he thanked Great-heart for all his help and charged him with relaying the news of his pilgrimage to his wife and children and to also tell them of Christian, Christiana, and their children.

The day Standfast entered the waters, the River was unusually calm, so much so that he stood in the middle and spoke with his friends, telling them how he had always been afraid of entering there but that the ground beneath him felt solid, and though the water was cold and bitter, he felt heartened by the thought of what awaited him. He told them of his love for Christ, who had sustained him for so long and who had been to him nourishment and light, guidance and healing; and now he was going to see him face to face. As he bid his Lord take him to himself, his strength faded, and he was seen no more.

The pilgrims ascend to the Celestial Gate—As the pilgrims ascended the hill to the Celestial Gate, they were greeted all around by a multitude of heavenly musicians, horses, and chariots, all welcoming them to the Holy City.

The narrator did not remain to see whether the four boys and their families crossed over, but last he heard, they were still living and spreading the legacy left by their parents. He ends the tale by saying that, should he ever visit that area again, he will recount what he sees. Until then, he bids us farewell.

About BookCaps

We all need refreshers every now and then. Whether you are a student trying to cram for that big final, or someone just trying to understand a book more, BookCaps can help. We are a small, but growing company, and are adding titles every month.

Visit www.bookcaps.com to see more of our books, or contact us with any questions.

CPSIA information can be obtained at www.ICGtesting.com
Printed in the USA
LVOW07s1605040916

503171LV00037B/1458/P